GUITAR

AN EASY GUIDE

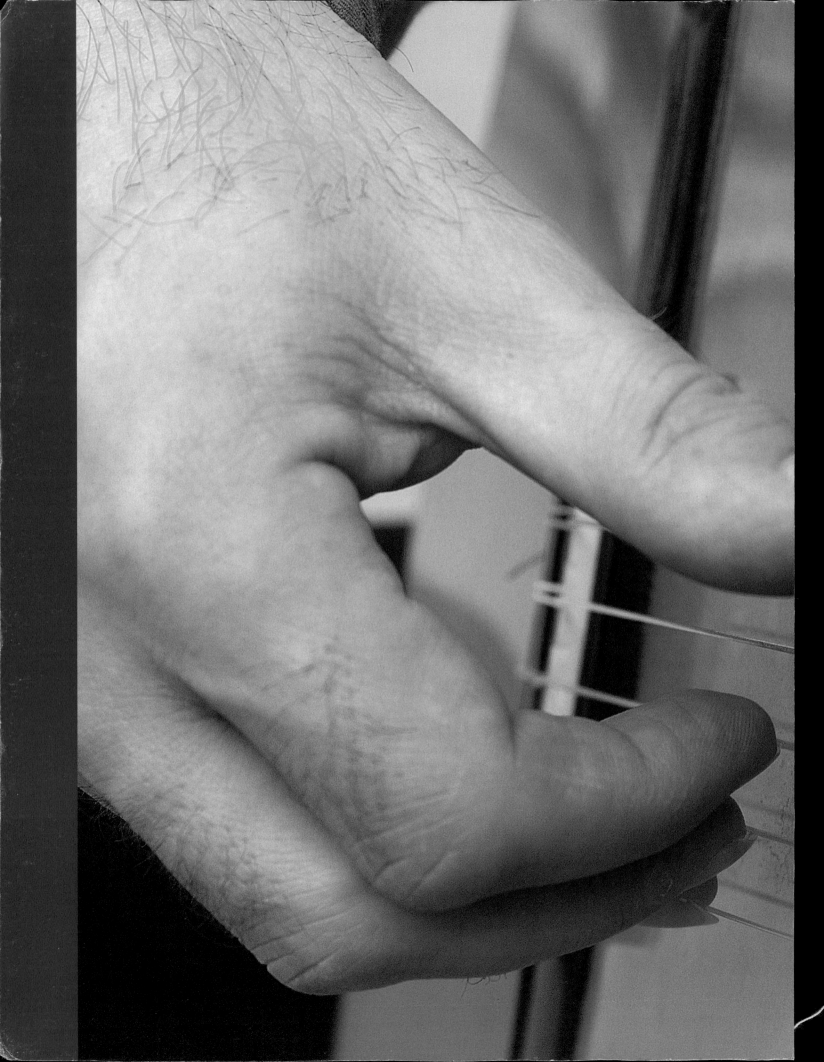

GUITAR
AN EASY GUIDE

carlos bonell

NEW
HOLLAND

First published in 2005 by
New Holland Publishers
London • Cape Town • Sydney • Auckland
www.newhollandpublishers.com

86 Edgware Rd
London W2 2EA
United Kingdom

80 McKenzie Street
Cape Town 8001
South Africa

14 Aquatic Drive
Frenchs Forest, NSW 2086
Australia

218 Lake Road
Northcote, Auckland
New Zealand

ISBN 1 84330 334 5 (paperback)

Publisher & editor: Mariëlle Renssen
Publishing managers: Claudia Dos Santos, Simon Pooley
Commissioning editor: Alfred LeMaitre
Designer & musical notation: Steven Felmore
Indexer: Leizel Brown
Picture researcher: Karla Kik
Production: Myrna Collins
Reproduction by Resolution Colour (Pty) Ltd, Cape Town
Printed and bound in Malaysia by Times Offset
2 4 6 8 10 9 7 5 3 1

AUTHOR'S DEDICATION

To the people of Carora, Venezuela, for their warmth and hospitality. To the staff of the Madre Vieja Hotel, Carora, for all their kindness and attention during the writing of this book.

contents

chapter one

TAKING UP THE GUITAR

THE GUITAR HAS A TWIN PERSONALITY — one aspect of it is firmly rooted in folk and popular traditions, the other belongs to classical music. Like twins, they are often difficult to tell apart. They have grown up together, sometimes going their separate ways, at other times coming close again. To understand their similarities and their differences is all part of the enjoyment of getting to know them.

The colourful history of the guitar encompasses troubadours, Spanish flamenco, courtly dances, great virtuosi, Gypsy jazz and much more. From a small-bodied instrument of four strings it grew to full size with six strings, capable of playing solo lines accompanied by an orchestra. Its players ranged from the mysterious figure of Nicolò Paganini to the Spanish maestro Andrés Segovia.

Stringed instruments have been around since the dawn of humanity — ever since the first human being fixed a length of creeper to a piece of curved wood to make a bow, and then heard with amazement the delightful sound produced when accidentally plucked by a stray finger. Depictions of people playing plucked stringed instruments date back 4000–5000 years. Harps and harpists are shown on vases found in Middle Eastern countries, in ancient Babylon (modern-day Iran and Iraq). Clay plaques from around 2000BC show a plucked string instrument with a body and neck.

Certainly the ancient Greeks enjoyed the music of the strings. The lyre, phorminx and kithara were three popular plucked stringed instruments of similar basic construction but varying in size and decoration. The word 'lyre' or *lyra/lura* in Greek was sometimes used as a generic term for all three. These instruments may have been related to the Middle Eastern instruments mentioned above.

RIGHT The shape of today's six-stringed guitar has origins dating back to ancient Babylonian and Grecian times, when early players plucked instruments with names like lyre, phorminx and kithara featuring anything from five to 11 strings.

ROOTS OF THE CLASSICAL GUITAR

Lyre

This was a portable, U-shaped harp-like instrument with a sound box at the bottom, and a length of wood or horn fixed onto each side of the box to form the arms of the 'U'. At the top the arms were joined by a crossbar. Strings were then fixed between the sound box and the crossbar, which were plucked using a plectrum or the fingers – the Greeks recognized both different techniques. The strings were of equal length and different notes were produced by using strings of different thicknesses and tensions. Depicted on vases and other ancient artefacts, lyres were often shown as having seven strings, but this was variable. Lyres were made in varying sizes according to the player. In later centuries the strings were also bowed.

Kithara and phorminx

The kithara was usually a larger and more ornate version of the lyre, played by poets, with a range of five to 11 strings over the years, while the phorminx was an earlier version of the lyre. One school of thought holds that the Greeks gave us the name of our modern instrument, the word 'guitar' being derived from the word *kithara*. Other similar words were in use in ancient times too – for example, the Assyrian *ketharah*. Both kithara and phorminx were played by epic poets such as Homer to accompany their verse and songs; music and poetry were sister arts in ancient Greece.

Ancient Egypt and Rome both had guitar-like instruments, and there are descriptions and depictions of such guitar-like instruments in Europe from the third century AD onward. However, there is little in the way of hard evidence at this stage of the guitar's history.

The history of the guitar is nothing if not complicated and controversial. Some people say that the Greek *kithara* was modified by the Romans into a more guitar-like form, which then spread throughout the Roman empire, eventually becoming the curved and waisted Latin guitar (*gitarra latina*), which was brought into Spain to become the direct ancestor of our modern guitar. Others say that the Arabic lute had a more formative role. The truth probably lies somewhere in-between, admitting many influences. And what is certain is that there has been a huge variety of stringed instruments over the millennia, especially in Spain where for hundreds of years Christian Europeans coexisted with Moors and Jews, giving rise to a fantastically rich cultural and musical mix. Turn to Chapter 3, p40 for a more in-depth account of the evolution of the guitar and its music.

Getting started

To get you to begin playing the classical guitar, the only essentials are a strung guitar! The rest can follow in good time according to your budget and how seriously you dedicate yourself to learning to play.

Buying a guitar

Set yourself a budget. A top-of-the-range, handmade instrument can be over 50 times more expensive than the most

LEFT The lyre (right), the kithara (centre) and the harp (left) were favoured string instruments of Ancient Greece.

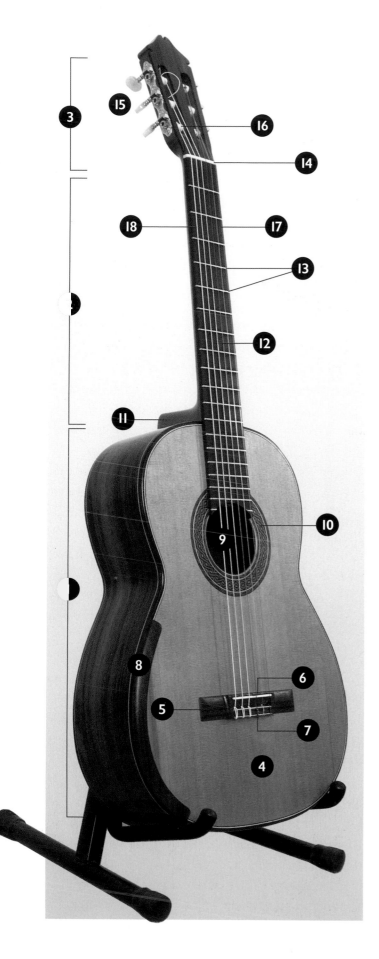

economic, factory-produced one, and there are guitars for sale at all prices in-between. The cheapest guitars are mostly factory-made. Expensive instruments are handmade using precious woods such as spruce or cedar for the top of the guitar and Indian rosewood for the back and sides, to improve tone and durability.

Find a specialist shop that will be able to guide and advise you. The specialist shop is also more likely to have a range from which to choose.

Take your teacher or a more experienced player along, if possible, to give guidance and advice.

Questions to ask yourself when choosing your guitar

Is this guitar the standard scale length of 65cm (25½in)?

The standard scale length is the measure of distance between the nut and the bridge, that is, the vibrating length of the string. A longer scale length means that the fret spaces are wider, and that you have to stretch further to reach other frets.

Guitars of shorter scale length, for example, 64cm (25in), are also available – and may be a good idea for people with smaller hands and shorter fingers.

Is it easy to play?

Note how much pressure you need to exert with the left-hand fingers to hold down a note, and compare with other guitars. Also compare the tension in the strings under the right-hand fingers when you play. Some guitarists prefer high tension, others prefer low.

1. body	7. tie-block	13. frets
2. neck	8. arm rest	14. nut
3. headstock	9. sound hole	15. machine head
4. soundboard	10. rosette	16. capstans
5. bridge	11. heel	17. treble strings
6. saddle	12. fingerboard	18. bass strings

Does it buzz?

All guitars, even expensive ones, buzz when you play certain notes very loudly – caused by the vibrating string rebounding against a fret. When you strike a string between the side of the sound hole and the bridge at a normal volume there should be no buzzing, or a slight buzz only on certain notes, particularly the G# notes at the 11th fret on the 5th string, 4th fret on the 6th string, and the 1st fret on the 3rd string.

Why does it buzz?

- The action (height of the string from the fingerboard) may be set too low. It is possible to reset the action, but this is a time-consuming process, since it involves removing the strings and saddle, replacing with a higher saddle (which may not be readily to hand), and restringing the instrument. If you are buying a cheaper instrument, it may be better to move on to another guitar. If you are buying a more expensive one and are particularly keen on this one, then you are strongly advised to take as much time as required to satisfy yourself that there is not something seriously wrong with the instrument.
- The strings may be low tension strings, and so are more likely to produce a buzz. Try putting on a set of high tension strings.
- The neck of the guitar may have been set at the wrong angle. An experienced eye can tell this if you hold the body of the guitar at eye level and look along the neck from the bridge end to the nut end. A person with an inexperienced eye may do the same, detect an uneven contour along the neck and blame the buzz on this factor.

  (Do take note, though, that many good guitars are constructed with an uneven neck contour along the fingerboard to facilitate playing, and indeed, to help avoid buzzing.)

Does it sound good?

- Listen out for the balance between the treble and bass strings, i.e. the relative volumes. Although the bass strings tend to sound louder on all guitars, they should not have an overdominating sound.

ABOVE The action – that is, the string height from the fretboard – at the 12th fret determines how easy the strings are to play.

- Listen out for the balance between the three treble strings themselves and between the three bass strings themselves.
- Check that all the notes on each string are fairly even in volume and sustain (see p90).

Does it play in tune?

- Check the intonation at the 12th fret on each string. For each string, the pressed note at the 12th fret should sound at the same pitch as the natural harmonic at the 12th fret (see also Chapter 5, p75) within a small margin of error. When you press the string down at the 12th fret on most guitars, even expensive ones, they tend to sound sharper than the harmonic. The margin of error should only be slight when you press the string with the left-hand finger parallel to the fret, provided that the action is normal.

  If you're not convinced by the intonation, ask the salesperson to change the string. More often than not, it is the string that is defective rather than the instrument.

- If after changing the string various times the guitar still sounds out of tune at the 12th fret, then there may be a serious problem with the construction of the guitar. The reason could be a warped neck, or miscalculated fret alignment. Avoid the instrument, and move on to the next one.

TIPS FOR BUYING A HARD-SHELL CASE

- Make sure the case is waterproof, and does not let in any rain. Examine the way the case closes to ensure that there are no hairline gaps.
- Check the weight of the case with the guitar in it.
- If there are ring handles on the case, these allow you to hook on a strap to carry the guitar on the back or shoulder. You may prefer this method of carrying.

Do you like the look of it?

You will live with this instrument for some time, so it is important that you like the look of it. Look at the different woods used for the front, the back and for the neck. Look at the colour and texture of the polish. Look at the design of the rosette, the headstock, the bridge, and of the heel.

What does it 'feel' like?

The overall feel is based on all the above factors together but is more than just the sum of its parts. It also depends on an instinctive response to the instrument.

Choosing a guitar case

The guitar you purchase may come with a case or, as the buyer, you may have a choice of cases. Rather like guitars themselves,

an expensive case can be many times more expensive than an inexpensive one. It is important that you buy a case appropriate to your needs and lifestyle because guitars are rather fragile and sensitive to weather conditions.

A hard-shell case offers more protection than a soft canvas case. If you need to carry the guitar long distances you may prefer the lighter, soft canvas case. Then you should find one that has thick padded protection. Hard-shell cases are available in plywood, solid wood (very heavy), and various types of fibreglass. Certain types of fibreglass cases offer the best protection, with manufacturers boasting that you can jump on the case, or drop it from a considerable height without causing damage. It's debatable whether the salesman would give you a demonstration!

If you intend to travel a lot with the guitar, there are two concerns you should bear in mind. Firstly, a good fibreglass case as described above is recommended for frequent flyers in the event that you cannot take the case into the cabin. Secondly, sudden changes of temperature and humidity can cause problems, such as cracks, splits and a contraction of the fingerboard. Again, a fibreglass case will provide some protection and is to be recommended.

Humidity and temperature

Changes of humidity can lead to expansion and contraction of some woods. Ideally, guitars should be kept at room temperature in a humidity of around 50 per cent.

In hot, dry conditions, keep a moist sponge in the guitar case. In cold weather, central heating and hot-air systems lead to a dry atmosphere, needing similar care.

Sudden changes of temperature, especially to freezing conditions, can cause cracks and splits. Take particular care in these circumstances. If you'll be stepping off a plane into a freezing temperature, wrap the guitar case in a blanket, if possible. The less weatherproof the case, the more you should consider this unusual action.

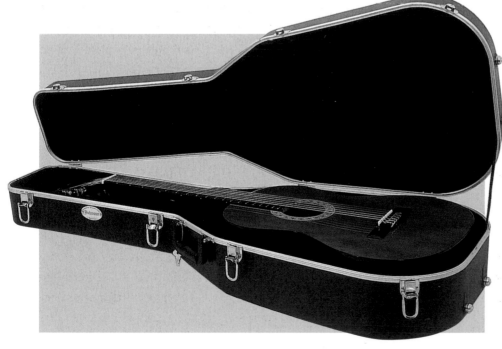

ABOVE The use of a humidifier is important in a dry environment to prevent cracks and splits in your guitar.

MAINTENANCE

The classical guitar requires very little maintenance since it has few mechanical parts and no electrical ones. Here are a few tips:

- Clean with a duster and a slightly damp cloth. Do not use any cleaning fluids or polish.

- Periodically, check that the screws in the tuning-peg boxes are not coming loose.

- Remember that changes in humidity can cause expansion and contraction in your guitar.

- Check the body and neck for splits and cracks. The reasons for their appearance may be as described on p13, or due to a faulty construction.

- Frets may need replacing if badly worn. This normally happens only after heavy-duty playing over a period of many years. Replacing frets is a specialized skill, and is certainly not a do-it-yourself job.

The strings

Classical guitar strings are made of nylon for the treble, and nylon-filament wound in silver-plated copper for the bass. They come in different gauges or thicknesses, and in different tensions, i.e. low, medium and high tension. For beginner students, low-tension strings are the most suitable, since you do not need to press so hard in order to hold down a note. Guitars with a low action may require higher tension strings to avoid buzzing. Conversely, low-tension strings may suit guitars with a higher action.

Changing the strings

▌ Thread the string through the front of the tie-block on the bridge – the front is the part closest to the sound hole.

▌ Loop it back and underneath the string at the point of entry.

▌ Hold the string in place against the outside of the bridge with the left hand, tuck the end of the string underneath the loop at the back of the tie-block, and pull tight with the right hand.

▌ Close the loop tightly against the outside of the tie-block.

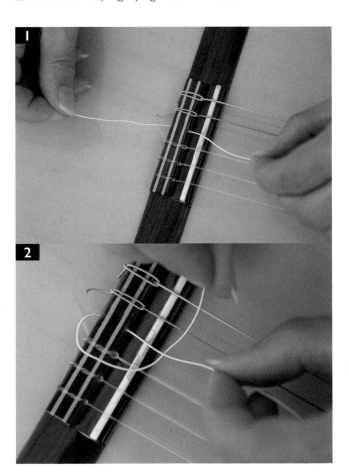

A-C Thread the other end of the string through the capstan hole in the machine head (the capstan hole should be facing you as you look down at the guitar). Tie as indicated in (C) and (D).

D To tighten the string, turn the peg anticlockwise. While turning, tuck the end of the string underneath the string going around the machine head, so that it holds fast.

Adjusting the action

The 'action' is the height of the string from the fingerboard, and this determines tone, sustain and ease of playing. Experienced players develop particular preferences and combinations. For example, some players prefer a high action with medium-tension strings since this gives a more percussive quality to the sound; others prefer a lower action with high-tension strings since this tends to give a better sustain (see p90) to the notes. Beginner students should play guitars with as low an action as possible, to avoid muscular strain in the left hand and arm. The best advice is to ask the shop to set the action to suit you rather than attempt to do it yourself.

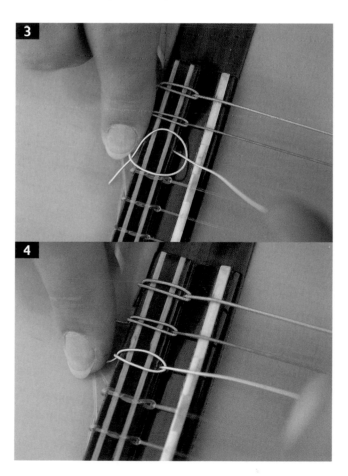

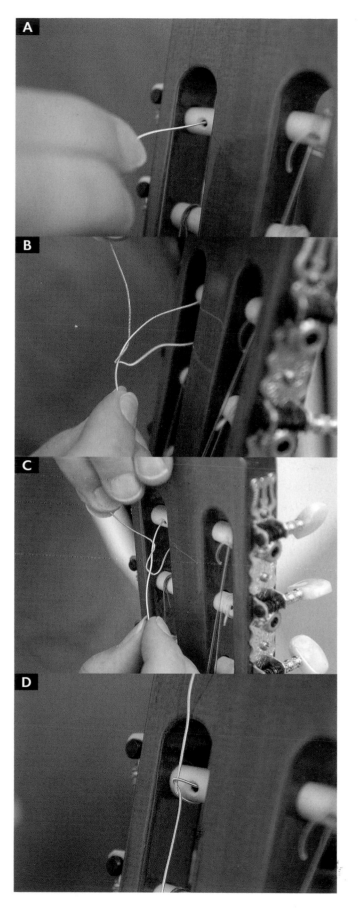

Nail care

If you play with nails, then you should keep them very smooth. Use wooden emery boards for shortening and shaping the nails of your plucking hand, and the smooth sides of nail buffers to even the edges and underneath the nails.

If you have difficulty growing your nails, or they break and chip easily, you may consider dietary supplements i.e. vitamins, minerals, and omega-3 and omega-6 essential fats. There are also special lotions that you can rub directly onto the cuticles. You can experiment with false nails, which may even sound better than your real nails! Specialist guitar shops sell nail kits that provide you with a set of false nails, glue, emery boards and other useful accessories.

Metronome and tuners

The metronome is a device that marks time with an audible tone or click, or visually with a flashing light, or both at the same time. You can graduate the speed to suit you and this will help you to keep time. The most reliable types are battery- or mains-operated rather than the traditional mechanical variety. Metronomes and tuners can be as small as a matchbox and as slim as a credit card. Most fit comfortably into a guitar case. There are various types of tuning devices – three of these devices are **electronic tuners**:

• The first type is specially designed for the open strings of the guitar. You set the tuner to the string you wish to

ABOVE AND BELOW LEFT Three types of tuners: pitch pipes, tuning fork and electronic tuner.

tune and play the note close to the tuner. It will indicate by means of a dial or a light whether the note is sharp, flat or in tune.

BELOW It is useful to keep a soft cloth handy for slipping under your strings and wiping down your fretboard.

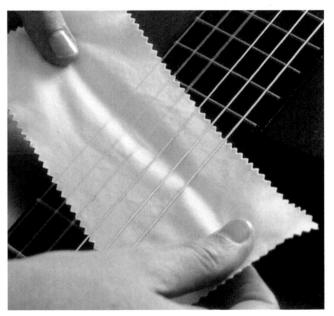

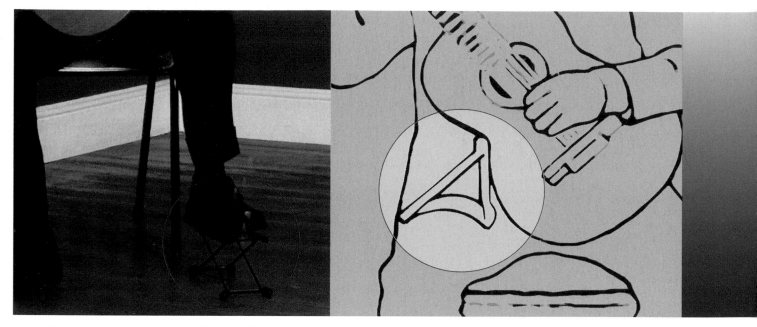

ABOVE The footstool is the more traditional of these devices.

ABOVE Height adjustment is more flexible with the *apoyo*.

- Another type sounds any preset note, and also indicates whether you are in tune when you play.
- The third is fixed to the guitar and automatically recognizes the string you are trying to tune; the tuner indicates whether you are in tune or not.
- **Automatic chromatic tuners** require no setting, and indicate the name of the note you play as you play it.
- The **tuning fork** is made to sound a note (usually A or E) when struck gently against a hard object. You tune by listening to the note and adjusting the guitar accordingly.
- **Pitch pipes**, one for each string, are blown to sound the relevant note. This is the least reliable method of tuning, since the pitch of a pipe varies the harder you blow it.

Footstools, cushions and *apoyos*

All these devices raise the level of the guitar neck to facilitate playing. Each has its advantages and disadvantages.

The **footstool** is the traditional method. You place the left foot on the adjustable footstool and adjust its height to suit you. Some people find this places strain on the back since, in effect, you are raising the hip joint.

Various types and sizes of **cushion** are available from specialist shops. It is placed on the left thigh, and the guitar is balanced on top of it (see photograph p19). The advantage is that both feet are on the ground, thus reducing the strain on the back. The disadvantage is that it may not provide the same level of stability for supporting the guitar as the footstool, nor are you able to adjust the height.

Apoyos are mechanical devices that are attached to the lower side of the guitar by means of clamps or suction, and then placed on the left thigh. The advantages and disadvantages are the same as for the cushion, except that there is considerably more flexibility in adjusting the height.

Capos

This mechanical device clamps onto the neck of the guitar at any fret. It presses down on all six strings, acting as a movable nut that alters the pitch of the open strings as you wish.

FINDING A GOOD TEACHER

Lists of recommended local teachers are sometimes provided by local or national associations, music schools or colleges. Although teachers may often have an impressive-looking string of qualifications, word of mouth can be the most reliable method of finding a good instructor. A good relationship between you and the teacher is essential for your progress and enjoyment. To this end, there are two questions you should ask yourself: 'What makes a good teacher?' and 'What makes a good student?'

WHAT MAKES A GOOD TEACHER?

A good teacher:

- presents learning material in an organized and gradually progressive manner. The material should be easy to understand.

- is helpful, understanding and courteous. Gone are the days of the proverbial rap on the knuckles when you make mistakes!

- understands your strengths and limitations, and works together with you patiently toward consolidation and improvement.

- should set you a clear programme of practice and goals to achieve.

- should have you feeling at the end of a lesson that you know more than when you started it, and enthusiastic about getting home to do some practice.

WHAT MAKES A GOOD STUDENT?

A good student:

- studies and practises in a methodical and organized manner.

- practises most days, whether it be five or 30 minutes, rather than a practice 'binge' at the weekend!

- is patient and courteous, and understands that the teacher may have difficulty in explaining material in an easily comprehensible way.

- is persistent in asking questions until all is made clear for him or her.

- follows the programme of practice and development agreed with the teacher.

- can help the organization of a lesson by declaring difficulties and desired objectives.

- is optimistic, but realistic, about his or her progress and ability.

ABOVE A good guitar teacher needs to work patiently with his student's level of ability in order for her to improve her skills. This student is making use of a cushion on which to rest her guitar, thus improving her playing posture.

chapter two

LEARNING TO PLAY

TO GUIDE YOU THROUGH THE PROCESS of beginning to play the guitar and learning to read music, the material has been presented in a sequential manner, so that information is supplied as it's required. In this way it should be easier to assimilate learning to play and learning to read in a co-ordinated way. Information and theory has been kept to a minimum, so that you concentrate on the essential information required to develop a basic understanding on which to build your basic practical skill. See Chapter 5 for more detailed information about theory, scales and chords.

Learning to read music, and to play directly from a musical score, is an ability that opens a door to a vast musical panorama. You have the guitar music of five centuries literally at your fingertips. The approach I have taken encourages you to learn to play and read music simultaneously, and so bring you closer to opening that door. For this reason, using tablature has been avoided wherever possible. Tablature is the graphic representation of the fingerboard, where each line represents a string. Numbers or letters on a line represent frets. Rhythms and fingerings may be indicated below or above. This method was standard for fretted instruments until the 18th century, and continues to be favoured over musical notation by many players and publishers even today — especially for styles other than classical. Although at the beginning it may be easier to read using this method, my observation is that players who begin like this seldom move on to become fluent music readers.

The surest way of learning to play with confidence is to acquire expert tuition. A good teacher will guide you through this chapter at a faster pace than if you try to do it alone. On the other hand, if you don't have the advantage of guidance, this chapter hopefully is easy to follow, and will guide you step by step toward a basic grasp of classical guitar.

RIGHT Carlos Bonell demonstrates the relaxed position to adopt when you play the guitar. Note the curving shape of the fingers on both hands, and the position of the thumbs.

PLAYING AND READING MUSIC

The following examples of the music symbols used in this chapter are based on a six-string Spanish guitar, which is right-handed, and with normal tuning.

Stave (or Staff)

Music is written in notes on a stave, which consists of five parallel lines.

Clef

The clef symbol at the beginning of the stave determines the pitch (the height) of the note. Most guitar music is written in the treble clef.

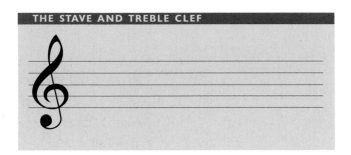

THE STAVE AND TREBLE CLEF

Pitch, semitones and tones

The higher the pitch of the note (e.g. a woman's singing voice), the higher it appears on the stave; the lower the pitch of the note (e.g. a man's singing voice), the lower it appears on the stave. The diagram above right shows the lowest note on the guitar (the note on the left) and the highest note (on the right).

Should notes go higher or lower than the five lines of the stave allow, leger lines are created; these lines are used only for a specific note.

The difference in pitch between two adjacent notes is called a 'semitone'. A difference of two semitones is known as a 'tone'. A semitone on the guitar is one fret; a tone is two frets. The difference in pitch between two notes is known as the 'interval' between the two notes.

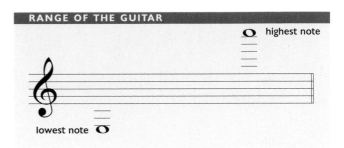

RANGE OF THE GUITAR

highest note

lowest note

Notes on the stave

Every note has a name based on the first seven letters of the alphabet: A, B, C, D, E, F, G. Notes are written either in the spaces between the lines or the line goes through a note. The illustration below shows the names of all the notes on the stave.

Time values

Musical notation indicates the time values (or rhythm) of notes, or in other words, how long an interval of time there is between two notes. The note with the longest time value is a whole note. A half note lasts for half the length of a whole note, and so on.

In the USA, notes are generally referred to as whole notes, half notes, quarter notes, etc. In the UK and elsewhere in the world, however, these same notes are traditionally known as breves, semibreves, crotchets, etc. The US notation is used here; however, you will come across the more traditional notation elsewhere.

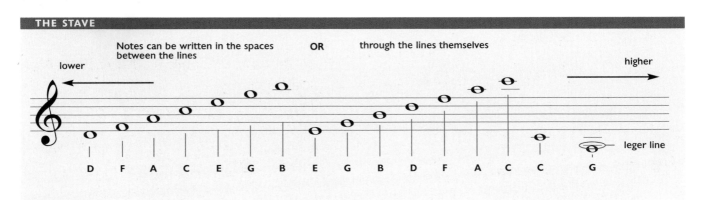

THE STAVE

Notes can be written in the spaces between the lines   OR   through the lines themselves

lower   higher

D F A C E G B E G B D F A C C G

leger line

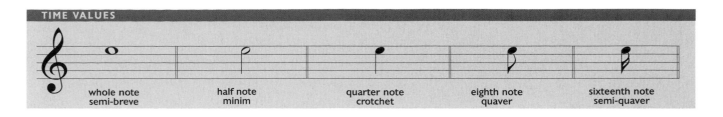

TIME VALUES

| whole note
semi-breve | half note
minim | quarter note
crotchet | eighth note
quaver | sixteenth note
semi-quaver |

Bars or measures

Music is divided into groups of notes according to the natural accent or beat of the music. Each group is known as a bar or measure, and the division between two bars is indicated by a vertical bar line.

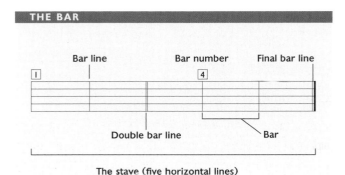

THE BAR

The stave (five horizontal lines)

Time signature

At the beginning of a piece there are two numbers. The top one gives you the number of beats per bar, the bottom number tells you the type of note for the beat. For example, the time signature 2/4 means that there are 2 beats in each bar, and each beat is

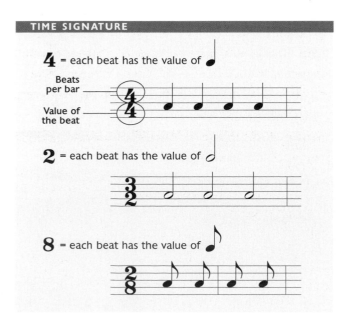

TIME SIGNATURE

represented by one quarter note. If you see the time signature, capital C, this is an abbreviation of 'common time', or 4/4. Here there are 4 beats in each bar, with each beat represented by one quarter note.

GUITAR SYMBOLS AND ABBREVIATIONS

Strings

In a piece of music, strings are represented on the stave by numbers in circles (see the illustration below). The string highest in pitch, furthest away from you and closest to the ground as you hold the instrument to play is the 1st string. The string lowest in pitch and closest to you at the top of the guitar is the 6th string. When you play a string without fretting it (without placing a left-hand finger on a fret), this is known as playing the 'open string'. The example below shows where each open string is on the stave, and the note of each open string.

Frets and the fingerboard

The fingerboard (or fretboard) is the playing area on the neck of the guitar which contains the frets. Each string can be played either open or fretted – the latter raises the pitch of the open string. When you play a string on a fret, you put your left-hand finger on the fingerboard, just behind the relevant fret; for example, 1st string, 1st fret, or 6th string, 5th fret.

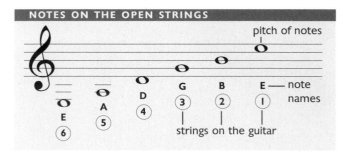

NOTES ON THE OPEN STRINGS

23

STARTING TO PLAY

Playing position

Sit on a flat-seated chair with no arms, your body inclined forward, back straight. Raise your left foot onto a footstool to sufficiently balance the guitar on the left leg, and bring the tuning pegs to about eye level. There are three points of support: the right chest, left leg, and inside right leg.

Alternatives to the footstool are a cushion or a support, all available as accessories from guitar shops. The cushion is placed on the left leg; the support is fixed to the guitar as per instructions. These reduce the chances of any back strain in some people, since both feet are on the ground.

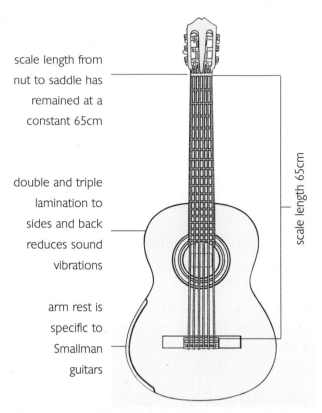

GREG SMALLMAN GUITAR

scale length from nut to saddle has remained at a constant 65cm

double and triple lamination to sides and back reduces sound vibrations

arm rest is specific to Smallman guitars

scale length 65cm

Carlos Bonell (left) plays a Greg Smallman guitar made in 2003 by the great Australian guitar maker. Among some of the additions Smallman has introduced to his guitars is the arm rest, which prevents the arm from having direct contact with the resonating body of the instrument; this avoids the vibrations dissipating through the player's body.

Smallman's most radical innovations are hidden from view, in the internal bracing of the guitar. Bracing consists of strips of wood stuck to the inside of the sound board to distribute the sound board's vibration. His lattice bracing is in a crisscross design rather than the traditional Torres fan-shaped bracing. In addition, the sound board reduces in thickness to less than half that of most other guitars, to little more than 1mm thick in places.

All-round, Greg Smallman's innovations allow a much greater vibration of the sound board, creating a louder and more sustained tone.

LEFT It is important for the quality of your playing to hold the guitar in a relaxed way, as shown here.

ABOVE The use of a cushion on the left leg allows the guitar player to keep both feet on the floor, thus avoiding back strain.

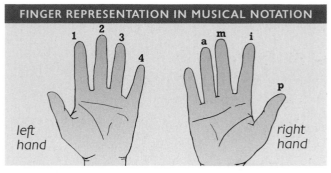

FINGER REPRESENTATION IN MUSICAL NOTATION

left hand

right hand

LH = Left Hand	RH = Right Hand
Left-hand fingers	Right-hand fingers
1 = index finger	p = thumb
2 = middle finger	i = index
3 = ring finger	m = middle
4 = little finger	a = ring

Tuning

It is strongly recommended that you purchase an electronic tuner so that you always tune accurately to concert pitch. To change the tuning, or pitch, of a string, first locate the appropriate peg. Place the guitar on your knee. Turning anti-clockwise as you face the back of the guitar raises the pitch (makes it go higher); turning clockwise does the opposite.

- Play the 6th string with your RH thumb, holding the string down behind the 5th fret with one of your left-hand fingers. Now play the 5th string open. The two should sound at the same pitch.
- Play 5th string, 5th fret with your thumb. Now play the 4th string open. The two should sound at the same pitch.
- Repeat this process on each string except for the 3rd string,

where you place a finger behind the 4th fret, instead of the 5th. The reason for this is that the interval between the 2nd and 3rd strings is a semitone less than the intervals between all the other pairs of adjacent strings.

Playing the open strings

Play all the open strings with the RH thumb in a steady, even tempo (quarter notes) as per exercises 1 and 2 below.

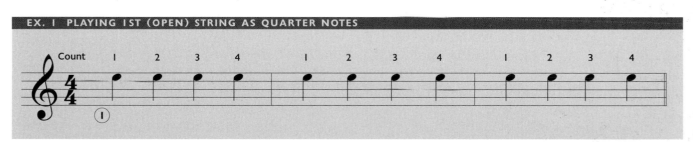

EX. 1 PLAYING 1ST (OPEN) STRING AS QUARTER NOTES

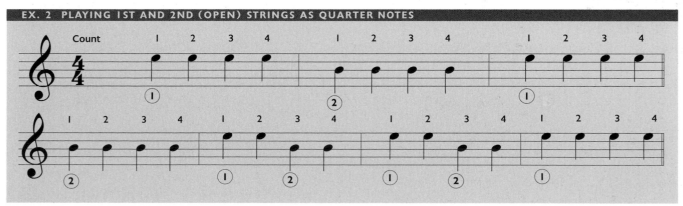

EX. 2 PLAYING 1ST AND 2ND (OPEN) STRINGS AS QUARTER NOTES

Changing time values

Remember that in 4/4 time, quarter notes = 1 beat, half notes = 2 beats. Play example 3 below counting aloud 2 steady beats per note. Next, try to mix the time values as per exercise 4 below. Keep counting aloud in a steady beat.

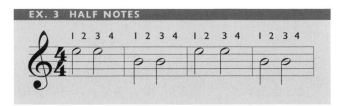

EX. 3 HALF NOTES

Then play 1st, 2nd, and 3rd strings (notes E, B and G) open as per exercise 5. (Notice that for the notation of the 3rd string, the note stems go up rather than down. Generally, the notes in the lower part of the stave have the stems going up, and vice versa. The reason for this is visual rather than musical.)

Try playing 1st, 2nd and 3rd strings open using different time values as per exercise 6, opposite top.

So far, you have played exercises in 4/4 time, that is, 4 beats counting quarter notes. Now you are going to play in 2/4 time:

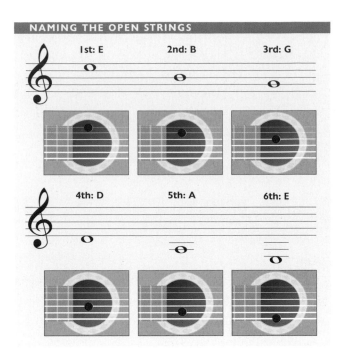

NAMING THE OPEN STRINGS

2 beats counting quarter notes. You will play on the 2nd, 3rd and 4th strings using two time values: quarter notes and half notes. The piece below is a simplified version of a Spanish bugle call.

EX. 4 MIXING TIME VALUES

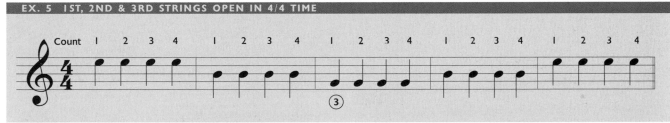

EX. 5 1ST, 2ND & 3RD STRINGS OPEN IN 4/4 TIME

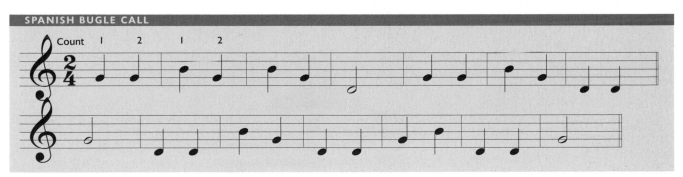

SPANISH BUGLE CALL

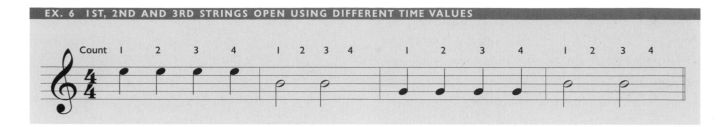

EX. 6 1ST, 2ND AND 3RD STRINGS OPEN USING DIFFERENT TIME VALUES

TECHNIQUE: RIGHT HAND

Playing across the strings

When you play across the strings, this means that you play adjacent notes on more than one string with the right hand. The development of a good right-hand technique is crucial for producing a good tone, and for acquiring agility, accuracy and velocity. So far you have played everything using the RH thumb. Now that you are familiar with finding the strings, it is time to introduce the other right-hand fingers. To adopt a good right-hand position you should do the following:

- Allow the arm, bent at the elbow, to rest fully extended on the guitar without hunching the shoulder.
- Allow the wrist to relax completely. Close the hand into a fist, and open it slowly, with the fingers curved. Drop the hand onto the strings.
- Rest the thumb on the 6th string.
- The wrist should be raised slightly, so that the hand is at a slight angle to the arm. This is to allow the fingers to move freely, and to create a more solid tone.
- Think of the movement of the fingers in three stages:
  (1) Preparation (2) Follow-through 3) Return.

Note that the index and middle fingers are always curved and stay in the same curve when they reach the string. As they follow through, there is a slightly increased curve at the middle knuckle (the fingers move from the top knuckle on the hand in order to produce the best tone). The 3rd finger moves in a straighter position because of its length relative to the other fingers, and the angle of the wrist.

Avoid pulling the string upward as you release it. You should press the string slightly downward as you reach it, and then release it as parallel as possible to the top of the guitar. When you have released the string, the finger should not immediately return but should follow through in the same direction.

Playing free stroke

One way to imagine the release of the string and follow-through is as an aeroplane taking off, just rising above the bushes at the end of the runway where the take-off represents

LEFT Play the bass strings with the thumb in an anticlockwise circular movement (as you're looking down at your hand), while resting the fingers on the strings, as indicated here.

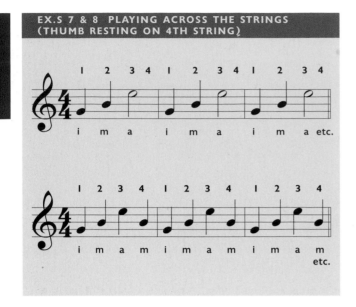

EX.S 7 & 8 PLAYING ACROSS THE STRINGS
(THUMB RESTING ON 4TH STRING)

EX. 9 PLAYING WITH THUMB & FINGERS

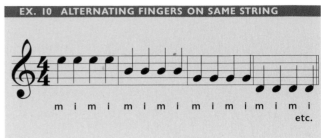

EX. 10 ALTERNATING FINGERS ON SAME STRING

the release of the string, and the rising above the bushes represents the follow-through. Now imagine your finger releasing the string and then rising just above the string behind the one you are playing. This right-hand technique is known as 'free stroke', i.e. the finger only touches the string that it is playing, follows through and then quickly returns to play the next note.

In examples 7 and 8 above, rest the thumb on the 4th string and play with the fingers as indicated in the exercises. Play in time, counting out loud.

In example 9, you play with thumb and fingers. After you have played the 4th string with the thumb, bring it to rest on the 5th string at the same moment as you play the 3rd string with the index finger, which will permit the 4th string to keep ringing.

Playing on the same string

When you play two or more consecutive notes on the same string, use alternating fingers; for example, the middle and index fingers. Agility and velocity can be most effectively achieved by alternating fingers rather than by repeating the same finger.

In example 10 above, play using the fingers indicated and rest the thumb two strings behind, on the 3rd string. So, for example, when you are playing the 2nd string, the thumb rests on the 4th string, and so on.

BELOW Playing free stroke on the 3rd string (left), and follow-through after playing free stroke on the 3rd string (right).

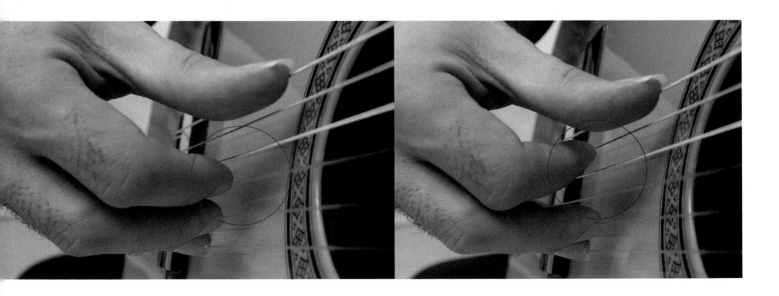

Playing rest stroke

So far you have been using free stroke, but there is another right-hand technique called 'rest stroke'. To play a note rest stroke, you approach the string in a very similar way to free stroke, but follow through by bringing the finger to rest on the lower string. You may find it easier to do this by slightly flattening the wrist, i.e. reducing the angle between the hand and the arm so that they are in a straighter line.

Rest stroke can be a more effective technique than free stroke to produce a firm, rounded and usually louder sound when playing two notes or more on one string or adjacent strings. Rest stroke makes a distinctly different sound from free stroke, and so is often used to highlight a particular note, or several notes, in a melodic passage. Ideally, you will develop a technique that combines both strokes, which permits you to alternate confidently between one and the other to be appropriate to the music you're playing and to the sound you wish to create. Now repeat example 10 by playing rest stroke.

Using nails or flesh

Most classical guitarists play using their right-hand fingernails. In this case, it is the left-hand side of the nail that comes into contact with the string, from base to tip, so it is important to keep the nails rounded and smooth. Others play without nails,

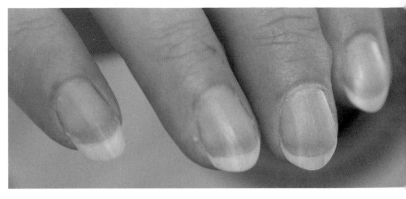

ABOVE Shape and smooth your nails for guitar playing using an emery board and nail buffer.

as did the great guitarist and composer Francisco Tárrega, so in this case it is the left tip of the finger that presses and releases the string. Otherwise, the technique is the same.

The use of nails or flesh will produce slightly different tones. If you have difficulty growing your nails, or they are weak or have an awkward shape for guitar playing, then you might consider playing without nails.

TECHNIQUE: LEFT HAND

The curve of the fingers in the left hand is very similar to that of the right. Hold your arm out in front of you with the hand palm-upward. Allow the wrist to relax completely. Close the hand into a fist, and open it slowly, with the fingers curved and the tips of

BELOW Playing rest stroke on the 3rd string (left), and follow-through after playing rest stroke on the 3rd string (right).

the fingers touching each other. Imagine that you are holding a butterfly in the palm of your hand, and that you want to see it, but not let it fly away. The fingers are curved at all the knuckles.

Now with the hand half-open, bring the hand to the guitar, place the thumb gently behind the neck and the tips of the fingers in line, in contact with any one string, without pressing. The thumb is placed slightly on its side, rather than on the flat, opposite the 3rd string. Place the hand so that the first finger is at the 5th fret, still with all the fingers in line. With the first finger at the 5th fret and the other fingers in line, allow the tips of the other fingers to extend, but only slightly. Adjust the position of the elbow and the wrist if necessary to allow the second finger to appear to be parallel to the fret.

Now observe the shape of the other fingers. Whereas the third finger is more or less parallel to the second finger, note that the first and fourth fingers are pointing slightly inward. This is perfectly normal and to be recommended. The only exceptions are people with particularly long fingers, or those who are double-jointed.

NOTATION

Notes in 1st position

When you place the left-hand first finger on the 1st fret of any string, the other fingers fall naturally on the following frets 2, 3 and 4. The name of the position in which you are playing takes

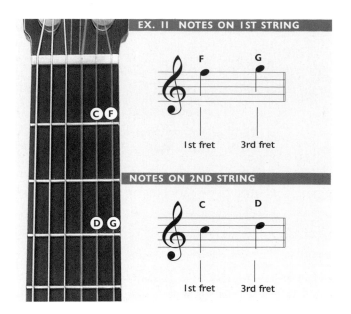

its name from the placement of the first finger. So in this case it is 1st position and here, for example, the third finger would normally play the 3rd fret. If the first finger is placed on the 2nd fret, then the other fingers fall naturally on the following frets 3, 4 and 5.

Since the name of the position in which you are playing takes its name from the fret placement of the first finger, your hand is now in 2nd position. As your playing develops and the music becomes more complex, you will begin to discover that there are many occasions when you cannot use such a convenient fingering arrangement – but for the time being this rule is a very useful guide to fingering.

Here, above, are some of the notes in 1st position. Remember the rule in 1st position: first finger plays 1st fret, second finger plays 2nd fret, third finger plays 3rd fret. In example 11 above, you only need the first and third fingers.

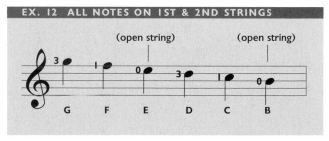

In example 12 above, the numbers next to the notes represent the LH finger, and the 0 represents the open string.

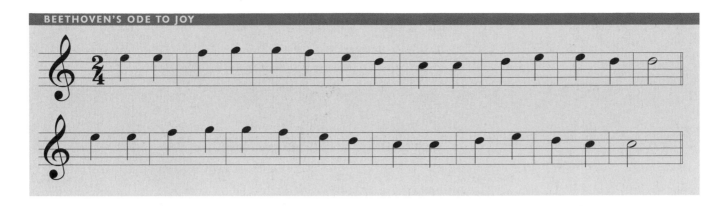

BEETHOVEN'S ODE TO JOY

Beethoven's Ode to Joy

It may surprise you to discover that some very well-known wonderful melodies have been composed using few notes in a simple sequence. With the notes you have learnt on the 1st and 2nd strings, you are now able to play the main theme from the last movement of Beethoven's Symphony No. 9. Once you have become familiar with the sequence of notes, try to make this sound like Beethoven intended – an ode to joy.

More notes in the 1st position (sharps and flats)

The symbol #, called a 'sharp', placed in front of a note raises the pitch by a semitone. Remember that a semitone on the guitar is one fret. If the # is placed in front of a note that is an open string, then it raises the note to the 1st fret. If placed in front of a note on the 1st fret, it raises the note to the 2nd fret, and so on. So far you have played the note G on the 3rd string as an open string note. In example 13 below you will find the same note but with a # in front of it, so you play this note, G#, on the 1st fret.

Similarly, the ♭, called a 'flat', placed in front of a note lowers the pitch by a semitone. Sharps (#), however, are more commonly used than flats in guitar music. These symbols are referred to as 'accidentals'.

So far you have played only consecutive notes using left-hand fingers, for example, E, F, G. Now play the following examples 14 and 15, which do not contain all consecutive notes.

EX.S 14 & 15 SOME NOTES NOT CONSECUTIVE

More time values

Eighth notes are twice as fast as quarter notes. There is the same time relationship between eighth and quarter notes as there is between quarter and half notes. Example 16 shows how an eighth note is written. A sequence can be written in two ways: as separate notes or joined-up notes.

In examples 17 and 18 you will find the same notes as example 16, but written as sixteenth notes.

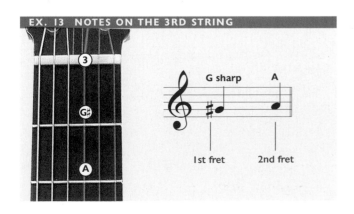
EX. 13 NOTES ON THE 3RD STRING

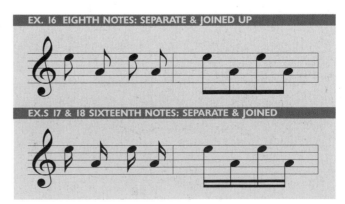
EX. 16 EIGHTH NOTES: SEPARATE & JOINED UP

EX.S 17 & 18 SIXTEENTH NOTES: SEPARATE & JOINED

Introducing 3/4 time signature

In 3/4 time, there are 3 beats in each bar. Each beat is represented by one quarter note. If in doubt, refer back to Time Signatures, p23.

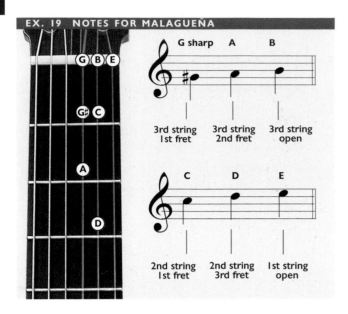

EX. 19 NOTES FOR MALAGUEÑA

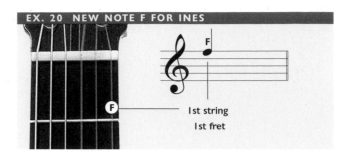

EX. 20 NEW NOTE F FOR INES

1st string
1st fret

notes in 3/4 time. Play very slowly in order to play fluently in time and without hesitations. Repeat as slowly as necessary, and as many times as necessary, until you have achieved fluency. Only then increase your speed.

Concentrate first on finding the correct notes with the left hand, no matter how you play with the right hand. When you are more confident, then introduce the alternating right-hand fingers technique discussed earlier (p28), using either free stroke or rest stroke, whichever is the easier for you.

Malagueña (Spanish traditional)

You now know all the notes required to play the theme of a piece of traditional music from Andalusia in the south of Spain. They appear again in example 19 in ascending order.

The theme below contains a mixture of quarter and eighth

Ines (Spanish folk song)

Here is another piece (below 'Malagueña') using the same notes, with the addition of the note F introduced in example 11 under Notes in 1st Position, and in example 20 above.

Note that 'Ines' is in 2/4 time, and contains half notes, quarter notes and eighth notes. To play this piece well, I can only repeat the same advice as for 'Malagueña': play very

EX. 21   ALTERNATING THUMB AND FINGER

slowly in order to play fluently in time without hesitations. Repeat as slowly as necessary, and as many times as necessary, until you have achieved fluency. Only then increase your speed.

Concentrate first on finding the correct notes with the left hand, no matter how you play with the right hand. When you are more confident, you can then introduce the alternating right-hand fingers.

Alternating thumb and finger technique

So far you have played everything either with the fingers or with the thumb. Now try alternating thumb and fingers (ex. 21 above). This means you can no longer rest the thumb on the 6th string. I have indicated alternating thumb *p* and index finger *i*, but you could also alternate thumb *p* and middle finger *m*. Move fingers only, keeping the wrist in a steady position.

Notes on 4th string in 1st position

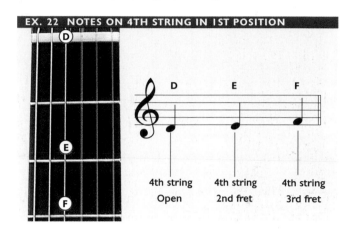

EX. 22   NOTES ON 4TH STRING IN 1ST POSITION

Malagueña (longer version)

The technique of alternating thumb and fingers practised in example 21 can now be put to good use in the longer version

MALAGUEÑA (LONGER VERSION)

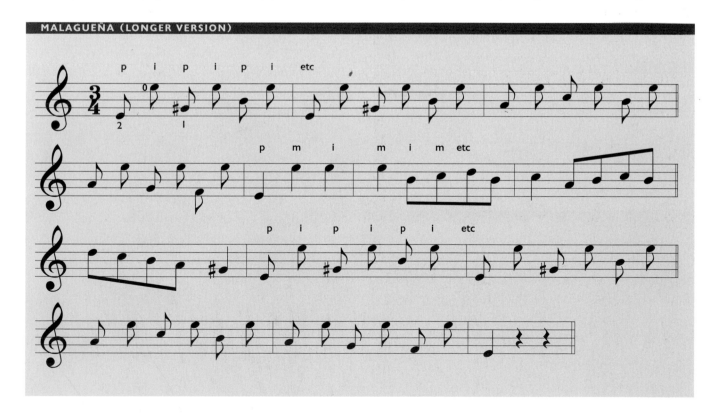

of Malagueña. Instead of playing the open string patterns of example 2l, you will be playing some stopped notes (notes on the frets) with the same right-hand string sequence. In the last bar the ξ sign is a quarter note 'rest'. A rest is a space in time where there is a silence. Two quarter note rests are necessary to complete the bar in 3/4 time.

Note on 5th string in 1st position

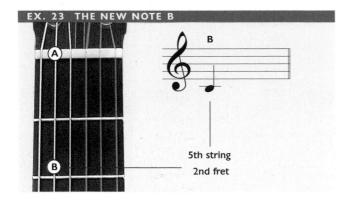

EX. 23 THE NEW NOTE B

5th string
2nd fret

INTRODUCING CHORDS

A chord is a group of at least three notes played together to produce a pleasing effect.

The E major chord

In example 24, the notes of the chord are written out in sequence from the lowest to the highest. Note that the chord only contains three notes – E, G#, B – which repeat at different pitches. You may wish to refresh your awareness of the meaning of pitch by referring back to p22 and p3l. To play the chord you will have to finger the note E on the 4th string, 2nd fret with the third finger since there are two notes to hold down on the 2nd fret at the same time. The second finger, which would normally play this note, is already holding down the note B on the 5th string.

Now, in example 25, bottom left, are the same notes written out vertically – when a chord or group of notes is played together, the notes are written in this manner. To play the chord, strum the 6 strings with the right-hand thumb.

The A minor chord

This is a similar left-hand pattern to the E major chord. The left-hand fingers are arranged in the same pattern, but one string higher. In example 26, the notes of the chord are written out in sequence from the lowest to the highest. This version of the A minor chord contains five notes, with the lowest note on the 5th string. It is followed by an example 27 showing the same notes, written out vertically.

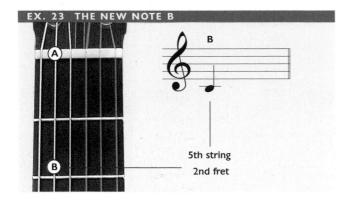

EX. 24 E MAJOR CHORD NOTES ON THE STAVE

EX. 26 A MINOR CHORD NOTES IN SEQUENCE

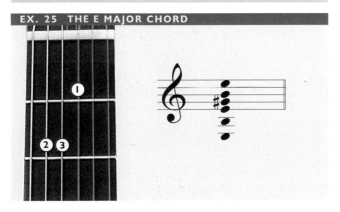

EX. 25 THE E MAJOR CHORD

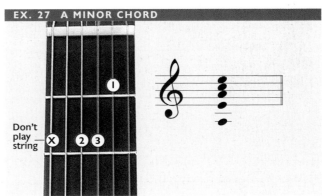

EX. 27 A MINOR CHORD

Don't play string

A SELECTION OF CHORD DIAGRAMS

D minor

A minor

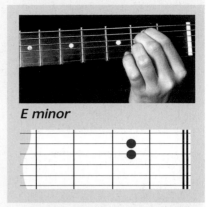

E minor

G major

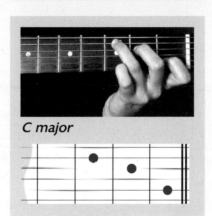

C major

F major

E major

A major

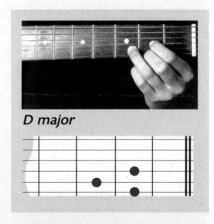

D major

E 7

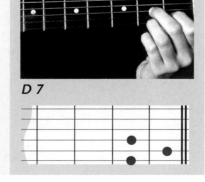

D 7

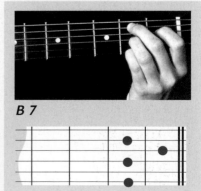

B 7

MALAGUEÑA WITH CHORDS

Melody, chords and harmony

In 'Malagueña' you played a tune which was unsupported by chords or harmony, although the section with alternating thumb and fingers suggested a harmony. This was because while you were playing a melody on the lower strings, you were also playing the repeated E on the first string. Almost all melodies in Western music are characterized by a harmonic or chordal support or accompaniment. Now try the elaboration of part of 'Malagueña' above, using the two chords you have just learned, E major and A minor.

HOW TO PRACTISE

An overview

A practice session is an alternation between playing all the way through a piece and detailed practice on short sections of bars or phrases. You play all the way through a piece to:

- establish the musical feel and shape
- develop technical strength and stamina
- gain insights and inspiration as to how you could improve the interpretation, no matter how simple the piece.

You practise short sections to concentrate the mind and fingers on creating fluency and accuracy. Here are a few frequent problems which can be solved by following steps (2) to (6) in the table on p37.

- You keep stopping at the same spot because you cannot remember where the next note is.
- The fingering pattern is difficult.
- You are finding it difficult to place all the fingers accurately to play a chord.
- Your right-hand fingers keep on playing the wrong strings.

At the end of a practice session, you should feel that you have not only enjoyed yourself but that you have also im-

Guitar playing is complex because, like the piano but unlike most other instruments, we combine melodies with harmony and chords. Most other instruments, such as the violin or flute, generally play one note at a time and so require the accompaniment of another instrument like the piano or the guitar to play the chords. The guitarist combines both roles in one, which is part of the attraction of the instrument as well as its difficulty.

If you have successfully negotiated the difficulties of the harmonized version of 'Malagueña' in the example above, then you have started on the long journey toward mastering the complexities of playing melodies with chords on the guitar. Whether you feel you are doing well or not, this may be a good moment to repeat the principles of how to practise, and to elaborate upon them.

proved some or all of the piece you are learning. To do this you have to strike the right balance between playing all the way through a piece and detailed practice on short sections of bars or phrases. The former may be the more enjoyable and appeals to the artistic side of your temperament, whereas the latter appeals to the more scientific and analytical side, and is necessary to the development of fluent accurate playing. The proportion of your time that is dedicated to playing or detailed practice is up to you. This will partly depend on what you are hoping to achieve in your guitar playing, on your ability to concentrate, and on your desire to improve, among other considerations.

How much should you practise?

In the early stages, 60 minutes every day should afford you time to enjoy yourself and to improve. Divide your time into three sessions of 20 minutes divided by two brief pauses, in which you put the guitar down, walk around the room, or do whatever you find relaxing.

If you cannot manage 60 minutes every day, then do what you can. Remember it is much more effective to practise something every day than save it all for the weekend!

Five-minute warm-up

It is important when you first sit down to practise to warm up the hands and fingers in a gentle way, just as an athlete goes through warming-up exercises before pushing him- or herself to the limit. These warm-up exercises can also serve as ways of improving your technique because they reflect basic aspects of guitar playing.

Left-hand exercise at 5th position

In a steady rhythm without playing, place the first finger on the 1st string, 5th fret, then the second finger on the 6th fret, third finger on the 7th fret, and fourth finger on the 8th fret. Now repeat on the 2nd string, and then on the 3rd string,

until you reach the 6th string, then move back onto the 5th string, practising until you reach the 1st string.

Right-hand exercise on open strings (free stroke)

In a steady rhythm, with right-hand thumb resting on the 6th string, play *i, m, i, m,* on the 1st string, then on the 2nd string and 3rd string, and when you reach the 4th string, release the right-hand thumb. Continue playing *i, m, i, m,* now on the 5th string and 6th string, then back on the 5th string until you reach the 1st string, resting the right-hand thumb on the 6th string when your fingers reach the 3rd string.

Right-hand exercise on open strings (rest stroke)

Repeat the exercise above using rest stroke.

Alternating thumb and fingers

Play the first bar of example 21 10 times, alternating *p* and *i*. Repeat, alternating *p* and *m*.

STEP-BY-STEP PRACTICE

The practising technique suggested earlier in the chapter should form a basis on which to build your fluency and skill. It is summarized as follows:

1. Play through the piece as best you can several times, even though there may be stops and hesitations.
2. Select a bar or phrase (group of notes that forms a unit) that is producing particular difficulty for you.
3. Play it very slowly.
4. Repeat as slowly as necessary, and as many times as necessary, until you have achieved fluency.
5. At the same slow speed, play again, starting from the previous bar or phrase.
6. Try to play it slightly faster. If you can play the phrase fluently without hesitations or mistakes five times in a row, move on to the next difficult phrase and repeat steps (3) to (6). If you cannot play fluently at the faster speed, leave that difficult phrase and come back to it the following day.
7. Reward yourself by playing through the whole piece various times, at whatever speed you like — whether you are making mistakes or not — and enjoy yourself imagining how it could and will sound like once you have smoothed over the difficulties.

Chords and arpeggios

- Play the notes of an E major chord, as in example 24, in a steady rhythm, using the right-hand thumb on the first three notes and then *i, m, a,* on the next three notes. When you play the notes of a chord one after another in this way, the sequence is called an 'arpeggio'.

- Now play the notes of an A minor chord, as in example 26, using the right-hand thumb on the first two notes and then *i, m, a,* on the next three notes.
- Play the E major arpeggio followed by the A minor arpeggio in a steady rhythm without a break in time.

TROUBLESHOOTING

Aches and pains in the wrists, arm, shoulders and back

You may be:

- practising by pressing too hard with the left-hand fingers. You need only apply just enough pressure for the note to sound properly, without buzzing;
- tensing the muscles in your arms and shoulders without realizing it. It's important to stay relaxed while practising and playing;
- sitting on an uncomfortable chair. The best chair is a flat wooden chair without arms;
- practising without taking enough breaks;
- inclining forward and hunching your back;
- twisting your body sideways, or twisting or craning your neck to view the left hand;
- supporting the guitar in an uncomfortable position.

To resolve the last three problems, refer to the Playing Position section, p24, earlier in this chapter.

Fingers feel stiff and clumsy

You may:

- need to do your warm-up exercises more slowly and carefully;
- be playing too fast;
- not be practising well;
- be tensing up (see Aches and Pains above);
- be trying pieces which are too difficult for you.

Many adult learners feel this way in the early stages. You may be expecting too much of yourself at this stage.

Making mistakes in the same places

- In your practice sessions, you may not be following steps (2) to (6) in Step-by-step Practice (see p37) with enough care or patience.
- You may be expecting too much of yourself. Progress for most adults is usually slow but steady. You can partly make up for the disadvantage of no longer having the supple muscles of children learning to play by using the analytical ability and self-discipline of a mature person!

Difficulty remembering where notes are

Revise the early part of this chapter to refresh your recognition of notes. A few useful tips to help you:

- Write out the notes on music manuscript paper. This will oblige you to concentrate on locating the position of notes on the stave, and to name them.
- Play the notes on the guitar without looking at the music, and name them.
- Play the notes on the guitar and visualize them on the stave.
- You can visualize notes on the fingerboard, name them, and visualize them on the stave, even when you don't have the guitar in front of you.

You cannot tune the guitar

- Buy an electronic tuner especially designed for the guitar. These are widely available in music shops. First try to tune your guitar without the tuner, then check the strings afterward using the tuner.

- New strings go out of tune quickly; they can take several weeks to settle. Changes of temperature and humidity can also affect strings within a few minutes.

Don't like the sound you're making

- You may be using a faulty right-hand technique with the fingers pulling at the strings rather than pressing and releasing them (see Technique: Right Hand p27).
- Your nails may be too long, or too pointed, or too rough. You need to keep them rounded and smooth to ensure a better tone.

- You may not be making smooth connected sounds because you are releasing the pressure of the left-hand fingers too early between one note and the next.

NEXT STEPS

You may consider taking a few lessons or joining a guitar society to receive advice and widen your experiences – which can of course include performing in front of others, either as a soloist or with a small group.

BELOW (From left to right) The author Carlos Bonell, guitar maker Greg Smallman, guitar maker Adrian Lucas (back to camera), and John Williams try out various handmade guitars at the Latin Quarter Guitar Festival 2004, in London.

chapter three

THE GUITAR AND ITS MUSIC

AS BRIEFLY DISCUSSED IN CHAPTER 1 (see p10), early forms of stringed instruments — the lyre, phorminx and kithara — were played in Greek and Roman times. Another stringed instrument, the lute, or *gitarra saracena*, originated in the Middle East where it was derived from the older Arabic and North African instrument known as 'the oud', or *al ud*. In fact, the word 'lute' derives from the Arabic *al ud*. The lute then spread throughout the Muslim world, and was brought to Spain by the Moors sometime in the eighth century, following their conquest of Spain in 711. After that, new instruments were brought across regularly until the expulsion of the Moors in 1492. One of these was the Moorish guitar, *gitarra moresca*, which was like a lute but with a longer neck.

Crusaders returning from the battles in the Saracen lands also played their part in the spread of musical instruments such as the lute, since many of these returning crusaders were troubadours who went along to fight. Troubadours were highly accomplished poets and musicians who travelled around the area of southern France, northern Italy and northern Spain from the 11th to the 13th centuries. Minstrels were popular entertainers — some were musicians, some performed acts such as juggling, and still others would have turned their hand to many of the performing arts.

Both troubadours and minstrels played the guitar and lute amongst a rich variety of other instruments. So we can imagine that many of the troubadours played the guitar on their wanderings, and the guitar again spread throughout Europe. At each stage, some forms will have become obsolete, with other forms continuing on and evolving.

RIGHT A painting by Dutch artist Jan Vermeer (1632–75), entitled 'Girl with a Guitar', portrays a typical Baroque guitar with double strings and an ornate sound hole.

LATE MEDIEVAL AGE c1200–1500AD

Royal patronage of guitarists, lutenists and other musicians certainly came to life in late medieval times, especially in the courts of Castilla, Aragón and Navarra, which are today regions of modern Spain. Alfonso X el Sabio – 'the Wise' (1221–84) – became king of Castilla and León in 1252. He was a great patron of the arts as well as a musician himself, and gathered many artists and musicians at his court. He commissioned musical works and published *Cantigas de Santa María*, which was one of the greatest collections of Spanish songs of medieval times. He may have written some of the music himself, others being troubadour songs. There are illustrations here of the Latin guitar, Moorish guitar, vihuela and lute.

At some point, the Latin guitar – *gitarra latina* – had come into medieval Spain, originating from Italy. This was the alleged descendant of the ancient Greek kithara (see also p10). It had four double-strings, which are also known as courses. The instrument had a waisted body, and was similar in shape to the guitar we have today. This four-course Latin guitar turned into the favourite accompanying instrument in Spain for the common man.

But for it to be used as a more virtuosic instrument, more strings were required. Aristocratic Spaniards added two courses to the Latin guitar to create a new instrument with six courses – the vihuela. Thus, they avoided playing the lute – which they regarded as the instrument of their conquerors.

Somewhere in the middle of all this evolution, a five-course guitar was also created, and became popular in the 16th century. This eventually became the six-string guitar we know today.

Meanwhile, the lute was the main fretted instrument in other European countries. The Moorish guitar was popular for a while in Spain as an accompanying instrument, but did not last – possibly because of its musical limitations, and because it was associated with the Moorish invaders.

So my theory is that the shape of the modern guitar was more influenced by the Latin guitar/kithara descendant, whilst the number of strings and its virtuosity was perhaps more influenced by the lute.

TOP This photograph illustrates the typical pear-shaped back and sloping peg box of the Renaissance lute.

LEFT An example of a decorative hand-written music manuscript from Medieval times. Each cultural period searched for a way to visually represent music – the first records of this date from the ninth century at a time when rhythm was as yet not annotated.

OPPOSITE In appearance, the vihuela differed only from this 16th-century guitar in terms of its six double-strings.

RENAISSANCE: A GOLDEN AGE

In many ways the Renaissance period represented the golden age of all fretted string instruments – except, arguably, the guitar. It is interesting to undertake a brief survey of the fretted instruments of this period, since the modern guitar has absorbed so much of the music discussed below into its repertoire.

The music of the Renaissance ranges from complex polyphony (the simultaneous combination of a number of melodic lines) in the style of vocal religious music, to courtly airs and dances of the most exquisite refinement and grace. This golden age starts for us in Spain, with vihuela music of astonishing quality published in the decade from 1535 to 1546 – and culminates in that glorious period of English lute music from around 1590 through to 1625.

Compare this to the guitar: the majority of publications that did appear during the 100 years or so from 1580 onward show little of the quality, musical invention and complexity of the vihuelists and lutenists, but instead concentrated on strumming techniques, simple chord sequences, and popular tunes of the time.

Largely due to this extraordinary quality of lute and vihuela music, and to the lack of musical invention in the guitar music of that period, the 20th-century guitar has 'borrowed' much of that early repertoire from its closest instrumental relatives: the lute and the vihuela.

Vihuela virtuosi: reflections of Empire

Among the earliest musicians, it is the published works of the vihuela players (or vihuelists) that reveal an amazing instrumental virtuosity. No wonder they were employed by the glittering Royal Courts of Spain to reflect Spain's newly found wealth acquired from its American colonies. Their virtuosity as

players and composers mirrors perfectly the confidence of 16th-century Spain in music of rapid scale passages contrasting with solemn, processional chord sequences and exciting variations.

The vihuela and its music

The vihuela bears a close resemblance to the guitar in the waisted body and flat back. It was strung with six pairs of double-strings, or courses, and with the exception of the third course, was tuned with the same intervals (differences in pitch) between each of the strings. This instrument was considerably smaller than the modern guitar.

The guitar of the 16th century was similar in size to the vihuela; it was also strung in courses, which, as we have seen, increased during the 1500s from four to five.

The lute, popular in England and Italy, had an oval-shaped back and was strung with seven to nine courses. It was tuned with the same intervals as the vihuela.

There was much in common between the early guitar, lute and vihuela. They were all played by plucking the strings with the fingers or the nails, not with a plectrum; they were all fretted; and to the untutored ear, they all sounded quite similar. What was very different was the type and the quality of the music composed for each instrument.

The outstanding vihuela composers Luys de Narvaez, Alonso de Mudarra and Luis de Milan published their music for vihuela between 1535 and 1546. Only Luis de Milan set out to write anything that we might today call a tutor, and that was the book he called *El Maestro* (The Teacher).

The lute and Dowland

The golden age of the vihuela and the Renaissance lute between them spanned a period of only some 90 years, from 1535 until the death of John Dowland in 1626, but within that

ABOVE Hand-written musical notation signed by John Dowland – the greatest composer of his time for the lute.

is willing to sacrifice some of the low bass notes on the lute which lie below the compass of the guitar.

Works such as 'Semper Dowland, Semper Dolens' (Always Dowland, Always Sad) for solo lute and the 'Lachrimae Pavans', which Dowland composed, arranged and rearranged for different combinations of instruments and singers, reveal an extraordinary artistic temperament, brilliantly projecting in music his own state of mind, and emotional state. Light-hearted solo pieces such as 'Mrs White's Nothing' and 'Mrs Vaux' Gig', probably aimed at the amateur player, make only modest demands on technique. Some of the fantasias, on the other hand, include complex polyphony and rapid scale passages, sufficient to tax the finest of players and clearly a reflection of Dowland's own abilities.

compass of time, music, the arts and indeed society itself changed profoundly. In the second half of this golden age, gone was the devotional-style polyphony of the vihuelists, and gone the more formal rhythms and harmonic progressions. Here now in music was exuberance, daring, improvisation, happiness, and despair. Here were human emotions quite separated from religious devotion.

In Italy there was Claudio Monteverdi and the birth of opera, revelling in emotions through music. In Italy, too, the scientist Galileo Galilei was demonstrating that the earth was not the centre of the universe, thus provoking profound psychological as well as scientific changes. And in England, William Shakespeare was born in 1564, in the same year as Galilei and only three years before Monteverdi. Shakespeare spent a lifetime taking his literary fine-tooth comb to human nature in all its remarkable manifestations. And one year before that, in 1563, John Dowland was born.

Dowland was one of the greatest composers of songs in the English language, arguably second only to Henry Purcell, his emotional range second to none, and certainly the finest composer of solo works for the lute. Fortunately all of his solo works for lute are playable on the guitar, provided the player

ABOVE Claudio Monteverdi (painted by Bernardo Strozzi in 1630) led the Renaissance in Italy. He composed the earliest operas, introducing the use of different-sized lutes in the orchestra.

BAROQUE ERA

Guitar music publications began to appear in the early part of the 17th century in Spain, France and Italy. They mostly contain much simpler pieces than the contemporary lute collections and tutors. Guitar books by Adrien Le Roy and Ludovico Roncalli contain popular song arrangements and dance movements, arranged as melodic lines with a bass line, sometimes alternating with passages of strummed chords. In France, the Italian composer and guitarist Francesco Corbetta under the influence of Lully composed and published more complex music in the emerging French style.

The Baroque guitar

Although Corbetta is recognized as an early pioneer of more interesting guitar music composed in the contemporary style, it was his student Robert de Visée who wrote the more memorable pieces. He, too, recognized his musical debt to Lully, in various arrangements for solo guitar of Lully's music.

De Visée (c.1650–1725) had a fine ear for the sound world of the Baroque guitar, which was an instrument of five courses, with the strings of the two lower courses often strung in octaves, i.e. separated in pitch by an octave (see p74). This is an effect similar to the modern 12-string folk guitar, but unlike both the lute and the vihuela. Bass lines of the Baroque guitar sounded simultaneously high and low in pitch, so creating a pleasing ambiguous effect, deliberately intertwining melodic passages with supporting musical lines. This effect was called *campanela* from Italian, 'bell-like'. Delicate bell-like sounds would contrast with the surprisingly sonorous effect produced by strumming chords. The Baroque guitar became all the rage in the French Royal Court from about 1650 with Corbetta and later with de Visée. Charles II, while still heir to the British throne, had taken refuge in the French Court after the execution of his father Charles I on 30 January 1649, and he too fell under its spell.

Spain and folk music

In Spain, Gaspar Sanz (c.1640–c.1710) published a guitar method with an anthology of pieces – original compositions and arrangements of popular tunes – which he called *Instrucción de Música sobre la Guitarra Española*. He concentrated on simple

ABOVE The introduction to 'Allemande' by Robert de Visée, from his Suite in D minor, written for the Spanish guitar.

melodic lines with a single bass-line support, and only occasionally wrote a few strummed chords. The tunes are catchy, memorable, never straying far from a folky feeling. It was music open to embellishment and improvisation by the player. Where once these tunes had been the province of popular music, now they had entered the more refined Royal Court.

Sanz, rather like Robert de Visée, played a guitar strung with five double-strings in the manner of the Renaissance lute described above. His advice was that for loud dance music, each pair of courses should be tuned to the same pitch (sound), but that for more melodic and delicate playing, each pair could be strung with strings separated in pitch by an octave. There are various implications here. Sanz may have played in a courtly band to accompany the courtiers when they danced; while they caught their breath, he would have played a delicate solo on the octave-strung guitar. Clearly he needed two guitars close by.

So, in the Baroque era, the guitar entered a higher social sphere. Looking at some of the great art of the day, the famous 'guitar player' in Dutch artist Vermeer's painting shows a well-dressed young girl playing a guitar in a comfortable house (see p41). The guitar is balanced on her right knee with the neck raised, and she appears to be holding a plectrum.

Baroque guitar and future trends

The guitar in the hands of de Visée and Sanz was beginning to develop a distinctive profile, or rather various profiles. Folk and popular tunes were transformed into solo pieces. More complex contrapuntal (counterpoint) 'art' music works were also included in their publications for the discerning wealthy amateur who would buy the books. And still the guitar would serve to accompany dancing and singing. The instrument had a proverbial foot in both camps, the popular and the courtly, which was to lead directly to the development of the so-called 'classical' guitar and the electric guitar of the 20th century.

Future generations of guitarists would build on this dual role: the guitar as a loud accompanying instrument in the form of amplified guitar and plectrum-played acoustic guitar, and the guitar as unaccompanied solo instrument seen in finger-style classical guitar and solo jazz guitar played with a combination of fingers and plectrum.

TRANSITION TO THE CLASSICAL ERA

At some point during the 18th century or earlier, the guitar began to change into an instrument strung with single strings. Scholars have tried to pinpoint the exact date but research keeps on pushing it backward in time – it may be impossible to establish exactly when that happened simply because guitars with double strings and single strings co-existed side by side. The huge variety of single- and double-strung instruments that go under names derived from guitars, lutes and vihuelas in Spain and the Spanish ex-colonies is witness to that.

It's clear that these instruments changed into something else, then branched off into other instruments, and each of these branches grew other branches. And so it was with the Baroque guitar, for it gradually discarded some or all of the double strings, added a sixth string, and also grew in size. At some stage during the 1700s, the six single-string guitar – almost as we know it today – was born, along with its first virtuoso performer and composer, Fernando Sor.

Rise of the virtuoso

Fernando Sor looks East

Soon after the French Revolution of 1789 and midway through Napoleon Bonaparte's victorious military campaigns throughout Europe, there emerged in Spain the brilliant guitarist Fernando Sor (1778–1839). Caught up as he was in the turmoil of Europe at war, and worse still in the invasion of Spain by Napoleon's France, he found himself on the wrong side of the conflict, and had to flee Spain. Although for Sor this must certainly have been a dramatic upheaval in his life, his subsequent travels through Europe, and his residence in Paris, London and Russia were to benefit the development of his chosen instrument.

His astonishing ability on the instrument was noted in all the salons and concert halls at which he performed. The best of his compositions reveal form, elegance and melodic invention, as in Andante Largo Opus 5 No. 5, the rondo from the 'Grande Sonate' Op. 22, the variations on a theme from Mozart's *The Magic Flute* Op. 9, and the 'Fantaisie pour la Guitare' (Largo) Op. 7. Sor's compositional inspiration was neither Spanish folk music nor the strumming techniques so loved by previous generations of guitarists. Instead, he set his compositional compass pointing firmly toward the Germany and Vienna of Mozart and Haydn. And his presence in London and Paris inspired a new generation of guitar players, who were able to witness a virtuoso at close quarters.

Sor was a great teacher who wrote numerous studies for students at all levels. Still in use today is his monumental *Méthode pour la Guitare* which he compiled in 1830, covering all aspects of guitar technique. An illustration from this book shows his recommended position of the guitar resting on the right leg, with the top of the tuning pegs at chin level.

The Italian connection

In Italy, too, virtuoso guitarists emerged, most notably Mauro Giuliani, Ferdinando Carulli, Matteo Carcassi, and the shadowy Nicolò Paganini. Giuliani and Carulli composed with great facility and they contributed hundreds of works for solo guitar. Clearly under the influence of Gioacchino Antonio Rossini, they excelled in exciting passages of fast arpeggios, and in creating the illusion of an orchestra in miniature. Giuliani's 'Grande Ouverture' Opus 61 is an excellent example, and sounds like the paraphrase of an imaginary orchestral overture by Rossini. Giuliani's outstanding contribution to the development of the guitar was to compose various concertos with orchestra, especially the 1st Concerto Opus 30, which contains some of his finest expressive writing in the slow movement. His series of *Rossiniane* are a virtuoso pastiche of Rossini themes which inspire the player to hitherto unknown heights of virtuosity.

Ferdinando Carulli, too, extended the musical environment of the guitar beyond the solo field by composing solo concertos with orchestra, double concertos with flute and orchestra, and duets, trios and quartets with a variety of string and wind instruments. Altogether, Carulli's compositional output exceeded 300 Opus numbers.

Carcassi travelled around Europe, living at various times in Italy, Paris, Germany, and England. He had a brilliant technique and wrote romantically inspired music – a forerunner perhaps to the next generation of guitarists.

Giuliani, Carulli and Carcassi were all renowned teachers who wrote inspirational lessons and studies for their students, with Carulli and Carcassi both writing their own complete methods. Carcassi also adopted his own, unique technique with which to

ABOVE Although Nicolò Paganini played and improvised brilliantly on the guitar, he never performed in a public concert.
OPPOSITE Ferdinando Sor was the first great guitar virtuoso and composer of the Classical era.

raise the guitar neck. In his portrait, Carcassi raises his left foot on a footstool, and rests the guitar on his raised left leg – which many classical guitarists still do today.

Paganini, a legend

And what are we to make of the man sometimes credited with starting the whole concept of the Romantic virtuoso? Nicolò Paganini was reported to be as good a guitar player as he was a violinist, yet he never played the guitar in public. First-hand descriptions refer to his ability to make the guitar sound like anything he wanted it to – and yet for the most part his many guitar compositions, in their simplicity, reveal little of this. One can catch a glimpse into a 'violinized' world of guitar playing in his Grand Sonata for guitar with violin accompaniment, where the guitar writing has some of the slurring patterns, fast scale passages, and high notes more usually associated with the violin, so creating an impressively virtuosic effect.

Where Paganini's contribution to the guitar is most impressive is in his chamber works for guitar with violin and viola, with string trio, and with string quartet. The best of these works suggest a huge compositional talent latent in Paganini which was never truly developed to its full potential. Although the role of the guitar is largely accompanying in these works, many contain a demanding solo − suddenly arriving from nowhere − jumping out of the thicker musical textures created by the bowed instruments.

Paganini, Rossini and Giuliani were colleagues and friends. There is a legend that all three once serenaded a young lady, with Rossini singing. Unfortunately the young lady never emerged on the balcony to acknowledge them!

THE ROMANTIC AGE

Francisco Tárrega

In 1852 a guitarist was born in Valencia, Spain, who was to have an influence far beyond that which his modest and retiring temperament might suggest. His compositions are few in number and mostly consist of one-movement miniatures. He composed no more than a handful of works lasting longer than five minutes. His playing was considered exquisite by those who heard him in private, and yet his public concerts were often plagued by nerves and self-doubt. His arrangements of music composed by his contemporary, Isaac Albéniz, set the standard for all future arrangements. And yet it appears that he never published any of his compositions until he was 50 years old. Afflicted throughout his life by ill health and poor nails, he experimented in playing with and without nails, restlessly seeking the perfect sound.

Francisco Tárrega (1852–1909) was born in Villareal, a small village on the Mediterranean. Here is a climate of hot summers with the sun casting deep shadows on the brilliant white village houses, and painting the sea in infinite shades of blue and grey and pink. The great Valencian painter Joaquín Sorolla, a contemporary of Tárrega, caught the light perfectly. And so did Tárrega in his music. 'Capricho Arabe' and 'Recuerdos de la Alhambra' (Memories of the Alhambra) are works which reflect Spain's strong Arabic heritage, as well as the Romantic idealization of the exotic East.

ABOVE There is a strong sense of Spanish romanticism in the music written by guitarist Francisco Tárrega.

Recuerdos de la Alhambra

Maybe no other guitar piece has so caught the imagination of listeners and inspired so many guitarists to take up the instrument as 'Recuerdos de la Alhambra'. Tárrega was inspired to compose the piece after a visit to the great Moorish palace on the hills of Granada, Andalucia − once the Moorish capital of Spain. The texture of the piece − the *tremolo* − has provided a constant challenge to players. Trying very hard to sound less like a guitar, and more like a mandolin, it relies on a constantly repeated note pattern played with the ring, middle and index fingers in rapid succession, with the right-hand thumb providing a bass line − which in this piece alternates between providing the main interest, a harmonic support and a melodic counterpoint.

The piece starts in the minor key gathering strength and shape as it rises and falls in pitch. Midway through, it modulates to the tonic major: a classic Romantic device which rarely fails to trigger a reaction. Tárrega times the entry of this effect perfectly in the piece – it is the musical equivalent of smiling through the tears. The return of the minor key provides musical balance, leading to a coda which ends with notes rising into the furthest recesses of the Alhambra palace.

Despite Tárrega's characterful Spanish music, it would be unfair to typecast him as only writing in this vein. The influence of Chopin and Schubert is clear in his preludes and mazurkas. The mazurkas 'Adelita', 'In G' and 'Lagrima' rely for their magic spell on a transparent expression projected through liquid sounds on the treble strings, and the occasional interjection of a melody deep in the bass strings.

Tárrega, Torres and the modern guitar

Early in Tárrega's life, the luthier Antonio de Torres (1817–92) provided the main impulse for further developments in the construction and shape of the guitar. Although the guitar had added a sixth string and discarded the Baroque double strings, the instrument had retained more or less the same dimensions. Torres's achievements were twofold: firstly, to increase the size of the body of the guitar (see inset photograph) and secondly, to incorporate a method of internal bracing (referred to as fan-strutting because of the shape) to the sound board, which greatly enhanced the guitar's depth of tone and sound projection.

Torres established the dimensions and construction of the guitar which became the template for most of the 20th century, and Tárrega was the first great player of the new instrument. His sound world could be described as follows:

- The spacing of chords with notes in the higher positions of the inner strings, sounding with an open treble string;
- Fingering patterns along the length of a string, rather than in the same position, to produce a consistent singing tone;
- Vibrato and glissando effects to enhance expression.

RIGHT Many of the piano works written by Spaniard Isaac Albéniz have been arranged for guitar.

It could be argued that the effect of Tárrega went beyond his quality as a composer. His music represents the Romantic Spanish spirit.

Albéniz, Granados and the guitar connection

Isaac Albéniz (1860–1909) and Enrique Granados (1867–1916) were also to draw inspiration from Spain's Arabic heritage and diverse music cultures, although in their different ways. Both composers were brilliant pianists who composed extensively for their instrument in a texture often reminiscent of and ideally suited to the guitar. This factor, together with the subtlety and depth of their music, encouraged Tárrega to arrange for the guitar works by Albéniz, including 'Granada' and 'Asturias'. Miguel Llobet followed with 'Torre Bermeja' and Granados's 'Danza Española No.s 5 & 10'. Segovia arranged more works including Albeniz's 'Zambra Granadina', 'Mallorca', and 'Sevilla'. John Williams arranged Albéniz's 'Cordoba' and Granados's 'Valses Poeticos'.

TRANSITION TO THE 20TH CENTURY

Pujol, Fortea, Llobet

Francisco Tárrega gathered around him a circle of devoted students, some of whom became concert artists, teachers, academic researchers, and editors. They included Emilio Pujol, Daniel Fortea and Miguel Llobet.

Emilio Pujol (1886–1980) combined all these roles. He lived to a great age, so that through his teaching and his devotion to Tarrega's technique and sound, the reach of Tarrega's direct influence extended into the late 20th century. Pujol's research into the vihuela repertoire led him to publish anthologies of vihuela music, especially edited with the modern guitar in mind.

Daniel Fortea (1878–1953) developed a notable career as a concert artist, but also found time to create an extensive list of publications in an edition which carried his name. It contained the first publications of his own compositions, his own arrangements and compositions by other, mostly Spanish, composers. *Biblioteca Fortea* set a pattern for other enterprising publishing houses to follow and build on, most notably the *Edition Andrés Segovia* for the music publisher Schott.

Tárrega's most outstanding student dedicated to a playing career was Miguel Llobet (1878–1938). Ironically, Llobet developed a technique based on nail playing, unlike Tárrega and Pujol. He belonged to the first generation of players who could take advantage of the new recording technology, which had been commercialized to produce 78 rpm records. These early recordings reveal a fine player, with a vibrato and rubato which we associate with players of that period. Pujol's playing as revealed in recordings, though, was quite different, especially in his interpretation of the vihuela repertoire which he championed.

20TH CENTURY: THE SEGOVIA REVOLUTION

Andrés Segovia (1893–1987) was born in Linares in Andalucia, Spain. There were no musicians in his family to guide his first musical footsteps. Instead, according to Segovia, in the absence of any classical guitar teachers, he learned what he could from the occasional visiting artist.

Although in later life he distanced himself from the flamenco guitar, claiming that he had rescued and revived the guitar from the café life where it had been relegated, there is some evidence that he did play the flamenco guitar himself as a young man, if only to earn his keep.

In the early 1920s he gave his first performance in Paris, to an audience that included an impressive range of composers and musical personalities of the age. He gradually established a name for himself, so that by the time he recorded a series of 78s in the 1930s, bursting with musical vitality and character, he had established his authority as the leading guitarist of his age. The arrival of long-playing records further enhanced his career and promoted his art worldwide.

LEFT The guitar arrangements of renowned guitarist Miguel Llobet were greatly admired by the young Andrés Segovia.

The Spanish Civil War, closely followed by World War II, caused him considerable personal and professional problems. During his lifetime he lived in Argentina, the USA, Switzerland and Spain, twice losing his home and possessions because of political upheavals. It was after World War II that Segovia consolidated his reputation with endless world tours and through his recordings, and rose to become one of the two highest paid musicians in the world, the other being pianist Artur Rubinstein.

Andrés Segovia's achievements are many and can be summarized as follows. He:

- set new standards of technical excellence;
- refined and consolidated a guitar-playing technique based on nail playing;
- played in much larger concert halls than guitarists had previously done, and so reached out to greater audiences;
- invited and inspired composers who were not guitarists themselves to compose for the instrument;
- created a guitar publications edition that carried his name, on which aspirant guitarists could rely for excellence.

Segovia's magnetic stage presence and playing made it possible for him to reach into the hearts and souls of his audience in large concert halls – no easy feat, since he refused amplification.

Encouraged by Segovia and inspired by his playing, composers such as the Spaniards Joaquín Turina, Federico Moreno Torroba, and Joaquín Rodrigo – as well as Polish, Mexican and Italian composers – all composed for Segovia and the guitar, with little or no previous knowledge of this instrument. One outstanding composer who *was* familiar with the guitar, was the Brazilian Heitor Villa-Lobos, a good player himself. Inspired by Segovia to compose a series of studies to complement Chopin's achievement for the piano, he composed *12 Etudes* which explored the full technical possibilities of the instrument, laying the foundations for a virtuoso technique.

The new Spanish generation

Manuel de Falla (1876–1946)

This composer once wrote that he never used real folk music themes, but preferred to invent them. Using flamenco-like fragments and themes, Falla reinvented Spanish music in the wake of Stravinsky and 20th-century atonality (the use of discordant sounds). Much of his writing in orchestral works

ABOVE Andrés Segovia popularized the guitar throughout the world as a result of endless concerts and music recordings.

such as *El Amor Brujo* sounds like a giant strumming guitar, with wistful melodies plucked out of an imaginary orchestral sound board. Falla only composed one piece for the guitar, in 1920: 'Tombeau pour la Mort de Debussy', edited by Miguel Llobet. This is a work of less than three minutes' duration, combining Spanish essence with moments of pure French Impressionism in the style of Debussy. It's one of the earliest pieces composed for guitar by a non-guitar-playing composer, and is one of the best. Falla based much of his early life in Paris, where various Spanish composers gravitated to study.

Joaquín Turina

Born in Seville, Andalucia, Turina wanted to transform himself into a more European-style composer, and asked Falla for advice and tuition. Falla's advice was that he should follow his instinct and stay within the Spanish firmament. And so he did. For Segovia, Turina composed 'Ráfaga', 'Fandanguillo', 'Sevillana', a three-movement Sonata, and other works, which never stray far for inspiration from the Andalucian flamenco music with which he had been surrounded as he grew up.

Federico Moreno Torroba

Less under the spell of flamenco, Torroba turned his elegant sense of form and style to a series of pieces inspired by the castles of Spain, and to a Sonatina which breathes the carefree air of Spanish skies. Andrés Segovia's guiding hand is to be heard everywhere in this piece, as in 'Burgalesa' and 'Nocturno'.

ABOVE Carlos Bonell plays to composer Joaquín Rodrigo at his home in Madrid in 1992. Rodrigo composed for Bonell, and the latter guitarist's recording of Rodrigo's *Concierto de Aranjuez* is highly acclaimed still today.

Joaquín Rodrigo

Of the four Spanish composers – Falla, Torroba, Turina and Rodrigo – only Rodrigo was born within the 20th century itself, in 1901, and lived until 1999, almost to see that century played out. His *Tres Piezas Españolas*, composed for Segovia, bring together various Spanish influences: the 18th-century 'Fandango' of Goya's Spain for the first movement; strident major second intervals bordering on atonality for the second movement 'Passacaglia'; and a 'moto perpetuo' (constant movement) 'Zapateado' for the last movement, which adds an insinuation of flamenco. These qualities reappear in many of his compositions, including in 'En los Trigales' (In the Wheatfields) – a brief work full of rhythmic syncopations (playing off the beat) and melodic fragments humming in a breeze blowing from the fields.

Joaquín Rodrigo was born in Sagunto, Valencia, on the Mediterranean coast only a few miles from Tárrega's birthplace. Partially blind from early childhood, and completely so later in

ABOVE Manuel de Falla, who composed slowly and meticulously, did not play guitar, and only wrote one (excellent) piece for this instrument. He lived for some years in Granada, Spain.

adult life, his music nevertheless is pictorial and descriptive of time and place. Like the great Spanish pianist-composer Enrique Granados before him, he was fascinated by the history of Spain, and in particular by the 18th-century Spain of Goya paintings, of courtly dances and of Scarlatti, the Italian harpsichordist, who wrote so many sonatas under the influence of Spanish harmonies and rhythms. One work, above all others, crystallizes the best of Rodrigo's music – a work that conjures the deepest soul of Castilian Spain in the slow movement, Mediterranean light and shade in the first, and an 18th-century courtly dance in the last. It's a work that was to define an image of the guitar in the 20th century, and proved to become one of the most popular concertos of all time: the *Concierto de Aranjuez*.

Concierto de Aranjuez

Joaquín Rodrigo, like Turina and Falla before him, went to Paris where he studied composition under Paul Dukas. Rodrigo met Falla there in 1928, and gave a piano recital in his presence which included his own works, among them 'Zarabanda Lejana' (composed 1926). Falla was sufficiently impressed to offer to conduct the work if Rodrigo made an orchestral version of the piece, which he did. Falla kept to his word. 'Zarabanda Lejana' was in fact the first piece that Rodrigo composed for the guitar, and then arranged for piano, before making a version for orchestra.

A decade was to pass before Rodrigo made another artistic connection between the guitar and the orchestra, which was to compose a concerto. Although guitar concertos had been composed before, no other Spanish composer of such distinction had set out to compose a Spanish concerto for the Spanish guitar.

Rodrigo began to compose the concerto in Paris in the late 1930s, while his wife was pregnant. Tragically, the pregnancy ended in a miscarriage. This event, together with the darkening clouds of World War II, following closely on the heels of the devastating Spanish Civil War, are often quoted as the inspirational backdrop to the Adagio theme of the second movement. This is not necessarily at variance with Rodrigo's explanation to the conductor Rafael Frühbeck de Burgos that the melody came into his mind while waiting at a tram stop. The musical flower blossomed in this prosaic spot, although the seed may have been sown at an earlier moment!

Rodrigo has said that the concerto was inspired by the beauty of the gardens and palace of Aranjuez, which was the

ABOVE This painting (1756) by Francesco Battaglioli of the gardens and palace of Aranjuez (inspiration for Rodrigo's famous concerto) hangs in the Prado art gallery in Madrid, Spain.

summer residence of Spain's Bourbon Royal Courts during the 18th and 19th centuries, including the courts of Carlos IV and his son Fernando VII.

The theme of the second movement Adagio evokes all these images. A steady pulse from the double basses, like a slow heartbeat, with the strings sustaining an almost unbroken line played 'pianissimo' (very quietly), provide the accompaniment as the cor anglais (a wind instrument rather like the oboe) and the guitar take the melody in turn. The trills and decorations of the tune as it gathers intensity are reminiscent of the Gypsy singers' improvisations in Seville during Holy Week. The solo cadenza (the unaccompanied solo guitar section) spirals to sweeping arpeggios across the entire range of the guitar, leading to an ecstatic orchestral reprise of the theme, a climax worthy of Tchaikovsky and Rachmaninov, and of Don Quixote proclaiming his love for Dulcinea. This is followed by a shimmering coda ending with high harmonics from the guitar and violins.

The Adagio *is* Spain. Later generations of musicians of quite different genres, including Miles Davis and Chick Corea, recognized this, and were inspired to compose their own varations upon it. The theme became a love theme set to words, in Rodrigo's own version 'Aranjuez, Mon Amour'. In the 1980s a pop version, complete with female chorus, entered the UK best-selling pop charts.

But there is more to the concerto than the Adagio. The first movement begins with a solo introduction by the guitar, strumming its way through an alternation of rhythms in two and three beats to the bar. The same musical material and rhythm is picked up by the orchestra, while the guitar takes a rest, only to re-enter and lead the orchestra for the rest of the movement. Brief, light interjections by the orchestra create a festive mood, like an idyllic village scene coming together, with Don Quixote in the guise of the tiny-voiced guitar taking the improbable lead against the orchestral windmills.

The last movement, marked 'Allegro Gentile', picks up from the first movement's alternation of rhythms, but this time we are transported back to a time of courtly dances, of Goya sketches, an idealized Spain of the 18th century. Flurries of flute notes and violin pizzicati (notes plucked with the fingers and not played with the bow) counterpoint virtuoso scales and arpeggios from the guitar. The concerto ends on three repeated notes played 'piano' (quietly) and 'pizzicato' at the octave by the guitar and the strings.

These 'piano pizzicato' notes that end Rodrigo's *Concierto de Aranjuez* can be heard as the hammer blows of the future that transformed the image of the guitar, catapulting it onto the world's great concert stages as a concerto instrument, and into the recording studios as one of the most frequently recorded works.

Agustín Barrios

In South America, a more relaxed attitude to the cultural division between 'art' music and 'popular' music is one of the continent's strengths, and there the guitar continued at the

ABOVE The Paraguayan Agustín Barrios wrote Romantic music of great beauty and harmonic complexity. His music effortlessly combined South American and European influences.

heart of popular music. It was into this environment that Agustín Barrios (1885–1944) was born. For art music, Barrios looked across the water to Europe – the Europe of Chopin, Bach and the Vienna of the Strauss waltzes. For popular music he had to do no more than step out into the village square, to see and hear *valses, polkas* and so many other local dances.

In the more popular vein, Barrios made virtuoso vehicles of such works as 'Danza Paraguaya', 'Cueca', 'Maxixe' and 'Aconquija', absorbing the popular roots of these pieces into his musical personality. Like all fine composers, he effortlessly integrated popular rhythms and melodies into a more complex Chopin-like harmonic framework.

Heitor Villa-Lobos

In addition to the *12 Etudes* composed at Segovia's suggestion (see p51), Villa-Lobos (1887–1959) also composed for the guitar '5 Preludes', 'Suite Populaire Brésilienne' and 'Chôros No. 1'. Villa-Lobos's contribution to the guitar was to create a repertoire in a post-Romantic vein, with elements of Brazilian folk music integrated into a highly idiomatic use of the instrument. Left-hand

ABOVE The prolific composer Heitor Villa-Lobos, whose work incorporated Brazilian folk elements, studied in Paris where he met leading composers of the day, including Manuel de Falla.

fingers press down chord shapes on the lower strings, sounding against open strings above, and slide up and down the instrument to create a kaleidoscope of shifting harmonies, some more dissonant than others. This has become a sound effect much imitated by subsequent guitar composers in different genres.

Heitor Villa-Lobos's first instrument was the cello, and many passages in his guitar compositions, for example, in 'Preludes numbers 1, 2, 4, 5' and in 'Schottish-Chôro' from the Suite, contain long flowing melodies on the bass strings, rather like the sound of the cello. His love for the music of Bach shines through in the Neo-Baroque sequence in the second part of 'Prelude No. 3', this time played in the upper register of the instrument.

The 'Suite Populaire Brésilienne' contains European dances like the waltz and the mazurka, filtered through a Brazilian lens to create a series of *chôros* – a melancholy dance in synco-

RIGHT US composer Igor Stravinsky pioneered a new kind of music in the 20th century – later termed the Neo-Classical style – and profoundly influenced future composers.

pated rhythm. Villa-Lobos's ability to 'Brazilify' Baroque, Classical and Romantic models knew no limits, reaching its apotheosis in *Bachiana Brasileira No. 5* (Brazilian Bach No. 5), a work for soprano and chamber ensemble, which was arranged for voice and guitar by both Villa-Lobos and Segovia.

The *chôros* rhythm appears again in 'Chôros No. 1', the first of a series of *chôros* Villa-Lobos composed for different instruments. Here the guitar plays by far the most conventional and romantic of the series. Overall, Villa-Lobos's eclectic range of styles and idiomatic use of the instrument, creating highly original music, had an enormous impact on the guitar.

20th-century music of a different kind

It is sometimes necessary to set an elaborate background for a real understanding of the intentions and inner meaning of a composer's work, and especially so with much 20th-century music. The first 30 years of the 20th century witnessed social, artistic and political upheavals which were to mark the rest of the century. Some of these changes were radical and profound, and still difficult to comprehend even today.

Various important developments began to materialize in music. Igor Stravinsky pioneered a way of reinventing Baroque music, which became known as the Neo-Classical style, by investing it with fragmented rhythms and angular melodies, but never straying far enough from the original models so as to become

unrecognizable. His ballet suite *Pulcinella* (1920) and his opera *The Rake's Progress* (1951) are excellent examples, as is the slow movement from Ravel's Piano Concerto in G major.

Schoenberg followed the logical progression of Romantic music into ever-increasing chromaticism (melody and harmony based on semitone movements). He devised a serial technique of giving equal importance to all the semitone

ABOVE Influenced by the European composers of his time, and also by the Neo-Classical style, Swiss composer Frank Martin succeeded in breaking away from the prevailing Spanish style.

notes of the scale, deliberately avoiding tonal centres and key structures which had dominated Western music for so long.

And so, having established such a background, it may be easier to understand the works of 20th-century composers who wrote for the guitar amongst other instruments. Some of these composers were influenced by atonal music, others by a less rigid post-serial Impressionism, and yet others integrated local folk music elements into their musical landscape.

Quatre Pièces Brèves

The Swiss composer Frank Martin (1890–1974) published *Quatre Pièces Brèves* in 1933. They are worthy of mention because of their striking difference to all other guitar music of the time, hitherto composed by mostly Spanish composers. A keen amateur guitarist himself, and immersed in the Schoenberg and Stravinsky European schools, he composed a set of pieces which make reference to both, and to the Neo-Classical style. The titles of the movements are taken from Baroque airs and dances – 'Prelude', 'Air', 'Plainte', and 'Comme une Gigue'.

'Air' is composed in a Neo-Classical style, with a slow fluid melody harmonized with Baroque-style harmonic suspensions, which are notes carried over, or suspended, from a previous chord into the next chord to create a pleasing dissonant effect. It also includes short and long trills which decorate the melody in Baroque style.

Frank Martin wrote that although he came under the influence of Schoenberg and serial music, he resisted it with all his sensibilities.

His *Quatre Pièces Brèves* show this, as well as the influence of Stravinsky and the Neo-Classical style. Martin broke with the Romantic Spanish image of the guitar, and created a new sound world for the instrument.

Guitar music spreads its wings

Although Schoenberg and Stravinsky each established their own template for the 20th century in the first part of that century, guitar music from the 1950s onward shows a wide range of styles and influences. The influence of serial, atonal and Neo-Classical styles continued but there also emerged inspiration derived from:

- modal music, which is pre-Renaissance harmony not based on major and minor scales;
- ethnic scales from folk cultures in Africa and Asia;
- jazz harmonies and patterns;
- The French Impressionism of Debussy based on whole tone scales;
- polytonality – the simultaneous playing of musical lines in different keys like Stravinsky;
- minimalist music – the repetition of small note clusters in gradually changing patterns; and
- post-minimalist music, in a return to a simpler, harmonic and sometimes quasi-religious style.

Some of the best music ever composed for the guitar, in the sense of harmonic daring, melodic invention and original use of the guitar's sound resources has occurred in this period. It has not all met with the approval of guitar players nor with the appreciation of dedicated listeners.

Only time will tell, as it has with the music composed by previous generations of ground-breaking composers, whether the music of composers such as Luciano Berio, Toru Takemitsu and Hans Werner Henze will enter the mainstream guitar repertoire.

Hans Werner Henze (b.1926)

This German musician composed *Drei Tentos* in 1958. They are three solo pieces from an extended work for tenor and chamber ensemble, and take their name from the Medieval and Renaissance *tientos* – instrumental pieces played by lutenists and keyboard players.

ABOVE Hans Werner Henze's guitar compositions include 'Royal Winter Music', inspired by Shakespearean characters.

ABOVE Sir William Walton and Benjamin Britten composed songs for tenor and guitar, and one solo guitar work each – both of which were written for Julian Bream.

Benjamin Britten (1913–76)

This English musician composed 'Nocturnal' Op. 70 for Julian Bream in 1963. An extended work of some 16 minutes' duration, it is played with scarcely a break, and demands intense concentration from player and listener alike. It is based on a song by the lutenist John Dowland (see also p44). The song 'Come, Heavy Sleep' is heard at the end of the work in Britten's own arrangement for solo guitar.

William Walton (1902–83)

Walton composed *Five Bagatelles*, also for Julian Bream, in 1971. It is clearly in a tonal language with harmonic jazz-like influences. Where the first bagatelle is in the style of Walton's own Symphonies 1 and 2, the second bagatelle sounds like an affectionate pastiche of Erik Satie's *Gymnopédies*.

Walton's *Bagatelles* were an instant success, not least because of the easy accessibility, for a listener, to a familiar harmonic language. Nevertheless, the facile exterior of these bagatelles belies an immense skill and wit in the writing itself.

Toru Takemitsu (1930–96)

This Japanese composer showed an intimate knowledge of the guitar in the various works he dedicated to the instrument, including 'Folios', 'All in Twilight', 'In the Woods', and for alto flute and guitar, 'Toward the Sea'. In most of these works, Takemitsu combined an oriental-sounding texture of isolated high harmonics, both natural and artifical, combined with sensual-sounding chords and discords, and a language reminiscent of Debussy's whole-tone scales.

Luciano Berio (1925–2003)

The Italian composer Berio wrote a series of *13 Sequenzas* for solo instruments, including the viola, flute, trombone, and guitar. He set out to create a virtuoso cadenza-like solo which would clearly stretch each soloist to the utmost, and to reinvent the instrument in a startling new image. For the guitar 'Sequenza XI', he chose to draw out of the guitar its explosive flamenco-like capacity in wild *rasgueados*, and multiple slurring patterns played only with the left hand, interspersed with the most delicate and fragile melodic snatches. The accumulated effect is one of ferocious energy alternating with exhausted calm interludes. The sheer animal-like energy it generates is breathtaking, as much for the listener as for the player.

ABOVE Toru Takemitsu's guitar compositions create an Impressionistic Oriental sound world.

RIGHT One of Luciano Berio's *13 Sequenzas* was composed for the solo guitar.

ABOVE Leo Brouwer, a world-class guitarist in his own right, has a great understanding of the instrument and has composed for the guitar since the 1950s, in a wide variety of styles.

OTHER COMPOSERS

Other major works are the Cuban composer Leo Brouwer's *El Decameron Negro*, and the Argentinian Alberto Ginastera's Sonata Opus 47. With the exception of Takemitsu, Leo Brouwer is the only composer of all those mentioned above who has a deep knowledge of the guitar. Himself a world-class guitarist, he has given to the instrument a large body of original works, with his earliest compositions dating back to the 1950s. *El Decameron Negro* was composed in 1981. It is based on the stories related to a German anthropologist by an African slave brought to Cuba in the 19th century. The three descriptively titled movements are: 'The Warrior's Harp', 'The Flight of the Lovers through the Valley of the Echoes' and 'Ballad of the Girl in Love'. Brouwer used minimalist techniques and pentatonic scales (five-note scales) to create a musical odyssey of great lyricism and beauty.

RIGHT Although Alberto Ginastera never learned to play the guitar, he once said that he had waited most of his life to compose for this particular instrument.

The four-movement Sonata of Alberto Ginastera combines atonal and chromatic elements, with the folky sound of the guitar of his native Pampas never far away. Like so many of the composers mentioned, Ginastera confessed to his reluctance to write for an instrument he neither played nor understood. Aided and encouraged by guitar players, these composers eventually wrote, more often than not, just the one work.

A more contemplative and spiritual side of the guitar was explored by English composer John Tavener in *Chant*, composed in 1984. This one-movement work rarely rises above a 'piano' dynamic, and was inspired by a Byzantine chant the composer heard sung in the distance, floating over the Greek hills, one hot day. The simulated sound of a bouzouki provides harmonic interjections. The work still awaits widespread recognition.

This brief survey of late 20th-century music is a reflection of the restless creativity of genuine artists that impels them to break new ground, to distance themselves from established precedents, and to challenge previously cherished notions.

chapter four

ACOUSTIC GUITAR – OTHER STYLES

ACOUSTIC GUITARS IN GENERAL PRODUCE THEIR SOUND from the hollow body, which acts as a resonating chamber. The main styles in acoustic guitar-playing, other than classical, that developed further during the 20th century include blues, jazz, latin, folk, and flamenco. The guitars used are many and varied in shape; some played with nylon strings, others with steel strings, some played finger style, others played with a plectrum, or a combination of fingers and plectrum.

While the guitar owes so much of its origins and development to Spain, the American continent both north and south contributed in large measure to its globalization as an instrument in the 20th century. In the USA there were radical innovations in guitar construction between 1890 and 1950 which were acutely responsive to the musical developments in popular music. In South America, outstanding musicians in Brazil in the mid-20th century launched an entire musical genre, the 'bossa nova', with the guitar both as its rhythmic backbone and main solo instrument.

The guitar has always had a foot in both camps — in 'art' music as a solo instrument, in popular music as an accompanying instrument — and during the history of the guitar, one or the other has occasionally been eclipsed by musical fashions and trends, leaving its alter ego to shine. Who would have guessed back in 1900 that here at last was the beginning of a century that would witness the confirmation of the instrument at the centre of popular music — as manifested in blues, rock, pop, and jazz — and that its solo exponents would become cultural icons and symbols? And the classical guitar was about to enter its golden age, too. First, we need to retrace our steps to the innovations in guitar construction that created the platform for the launch of this phenomenon.

RIGHT Sting — formerly of the rock band The Police — has, as a musician in his own right, embraced many different styles and influences during a lengthy solo career. Here he plays Spanish guitar at one of his concerts.

STYLES & INFLUENCES

New World guitar makers

The luthier Antonio de Torres in Spain was not the only guitar maker rethinking the shape and structure of guitars in the mid-19th century. Christian Frederick Martin, who was born in Germany, was doing the same in the USA. He, too, enlarged the body shape of the guitar (manufactured as the 'OO' model), and increased it further in the 1870s (the 'OOO' model), both with a finger plate and a characteristic belly-shaped bridge. The effect was to increase the volume and improve the playability of the instrument. This suited the blues players and singers growing up mostly in the Deep South of the USA, who gradually took to the guitar as their main accompanying instrument.

Orville Gibson, born in the USA, took guitar construction several stages further. In the 1890s he developed an arch-top guitar whose construction principles were based on the violin, with an oval-shaped sound hole. He also pioneered stringing with steel in place of gut strings. These developments further enhanced the sound of the guitar, with steel strings a perfect vehicle for chordal accompaniments and penetrating solo lines.

Blues and jazz

Outstanding early blues guitar players included Robert Johnson, pioneer of the acoustic bottleneck slide. This consisted of sliding a small piece of glass or metal placed on one finger across the strings, to produce a fretless singing sound. The style was referred to as the Delta Blues, which owed its origins to the Mississippi Delta, where in 1900 slavery was still within living memory and experience. Blues music and blues guitar grew from this background. Robert Johnson sang and accompanied himself. Solo guitar lines would punctuate the verses in lament-like improvisations rather in the style of the flamenco songs of the deep south of Spain.

The earliest jazz was played in small groups with the banjo, not the guitar, as the main accompanying instrument. Gradually, the small groups became larger, so that by the 1930s they were 'big bands'. At the forefront were the bands of Duke Ellington, Count Basie and Benny Goodman. The rhythm sections also grew larger to include piano, bass, guitar, and drums. The guitar had ousted the banjo as the main string instrument. All this may not have been possible without the radical changes that Orville Gibson introduced to guitar construction, permitting a much louder sound.

Only one more step was required to truly emancipate the guitar, which was to endow it with a level of volume equal to that of the other instruments. This was the electromagnetic pick-up that amplified the sound of the instrument through a speaker, and which appeared in the early 1930s.

And so a new generation of guitar virtuosi, who played and improvised solos with a backing band, was ushered in. Charlie Christian is acknowledged as the first great player of this type of guitar, to be precise an Electric Spanish Gibson ES-150. This was a guitar with F-holes rather than a rounded or oval-shaped sound hole.

ABOVE The legendary Charlie Christian was one of the first guitarists to 'solo' in front of a band.

INSET The Gibson L-5 (1924) was designed with two f-holes in place of an oval sound hole; it all but replaced the banjo.

12-BAR BLUES SEQUENCE IN C

BLUES TURNAROUNDS (3 EXAMPLES)

Charlie Christian (c.1919–42) was born in Dallas, Texas, and came from a musical family. His interest in musical instruments was such that he learned to play the trumpet, acoustic guitar, double bass, and piano. He joined the Benny Goodman quintet for one engagement in 1939, which was such a success that the quintet became a sextet. He also played and recorded as soloist with the Benny Goodman Orchestra, until his untimely death in 1942. Charlie Christian is regarded as the first great guitarist to play solo in front of a band, and as one of the founders of 'bebop' jazz. Not since Renaissance times and the golden age of the lute, had a plucked-instrument player been at the forefront of developments in any musical style.

Django Reinhardt and Gypsy jazz

Almost at the same time, another guitarist was fronting a quintet on the other side of the Atlantic, in an even more unusual reversal of roles. He, too, was playing an acoustic guitar, but in his case, without amplification.

The band was the Quintette du Hot Club de France and included Stephane Grappelli on violin, who traded solos with Django Reinhardt, and when accompanying, played long sooth-

ABOVE Django Reinhardt (second from left) playing in Paris with the Quintette du Hot Club de France. Stephane Grappelli is playing the violin, second from right.

ing lines against the guitar's staccato scales. Reinhardt must take the prize as the most improbable guitar hero of all time.

Born into a Belgian Gypsy family, Django Reinhardt (1910–53) did not visit the USA until he was in his late twenties. Due to an accident, he was unable to use the third and fourth fingers of his left hand. He could not read music. And yet his musical invention and improvisations were astonishing. His technical prowess, in spite of his disability, was second to none. The expressive range of his playing included ballads played with delicacy and a characteristic vibrato through to extremely fast passages, some played in octaves, interspersed with rhythmic accompaniments that frequently distracted attention from the main tune.

Django's jazz style is referred to as 'Gypsy jazz'. It is hard to disentangle the various strands of his brilliance, but chief among them are his ability to create the sounds of a big band in his chord playing, his sense of timing and rhythm, and his unmistakable quality of sound.

He played a guitar made by the Italian maker, Mario Maccaferri, who produced guitars for the Paris-based Selmer company in the early 1930s. It had a body cutaway, a D-shaped sound hole, extra frets on the top string, a metal tailpiece, a flat top, and an internal resonating chamber within the soundbox.

Both Charlie Christian and Django Reinhardt played acoustic guitars. These artists were among the last great players who grew up with only this type of guitar – but also the first generation to use the electromagnetic pick-up. Django lived to see and play the next great invention, although Charlie Christian did not. That invention was the development of the solid-body guitar with pick-up, where this guitar type relies entirely on amplification for its sound. By 1950, the Fender Company was mass-producing a solid-body electric guitar with a cutaway. The Gibson Company followed suit in 1952. The guitar family tree had grown another branch, whose radically different method of sound production distanced it from the trunk like no other branch before it!

João Gilberto and bossa nova

Aware of these developments, but still preferring the traditional sound of the acoustic guitar, a group of musicians in Latin America were making a profound impact on jazz and the musical culture of the time. With the guitar as his chosen instrument, singer-guitarist João Gilberto (b.1931) developed the 'bossa nova' style in Brazil along with pianist-composer Antonio Carlos Jobim.

Bossa nova, which means 'new wave', started in Rio de Janeiro. It integrates European, African and native American elements seamlessly into a highly sophisticated melodic, harmonic and rhythmic design. Its most striking features to the listener are the irresistible syncopated rhythms: sometimes slow, sometimes fast, but never frantic or furious like so much other 20th-century music including much jazz repertoire. 'The Girl from Ipanema' and

RIGHT Despite his disability, Django Reinhardt was one of the greatest guitarists of the 20th century.

DJANGO'S GYPSY JAZZ

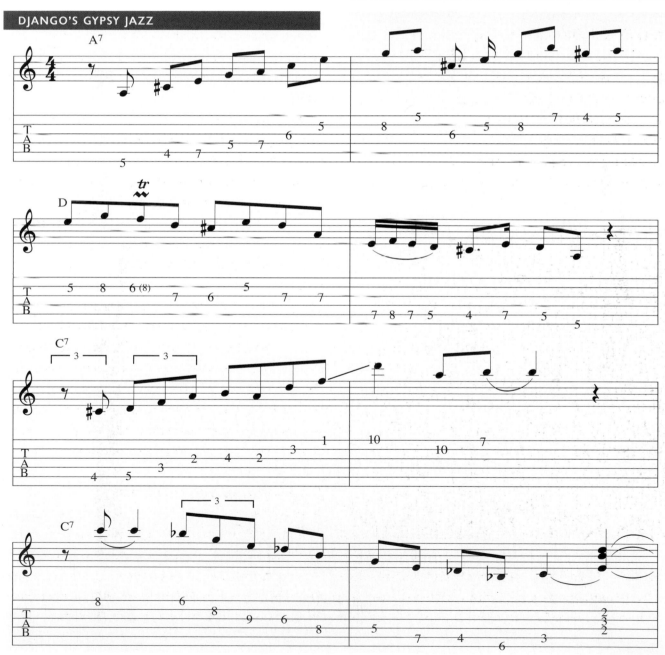

'Desafinado' are outstanding examples of this style, and became major international hits. An indefinably relaxed style permeates bossa nova, reflecting a music of unusual gentleness. João Gilberto's guitar-playing accompaniments are characterized by melodic-sounding chord progressions. When he accompanies himself singing he produces complex guitar playing, which is extremely demanding to achieve. The bossa nova guitar style integrates melody, harmony and rhythm into an expressive style of great beauty which has deeply affected and influenced jazz. Like Charlie Christian before him, Gilberto profoundly influenced the development of a generic musical style on the American continent.

BOSSA NOVA

ABOVE The development of the bossa nova style, which started in Latin America, is in large part due to João Gilberto – singer, guitarist and composer.

From folk to pop and rock

Centuries of folk music found fertile ground for further growth in the USA, with its immigrants from all over the world who brought their traditions with them. Together with the innovations of Martin and Gibson, these were two important factors that led to the explosive growth of the guitar as an accompanying instrument during the 20th century.

There are now many thousands of singer-songwriters worldwide who accompany themselves on the acoustic guitar, using both finger-style and plectrum techniques. This started off as folk music but has now branched off to include other styles as well, especially the pop music of the late 20th century and into the 21st.

Perhaps the first great figure in US 20th-century folk music was Woody Guthrie (1912–67), who travelled the USA writing and singing his songs, many of which are now folk classic – for example, 'This Land is your Land'. He had great sympathy with immigrants and low-paid workers, and wrote many songs specifically for them, including early 'protest' songs about

RIGHT Bob Dylan wasn't afraid to move with the times, and became adept at playing both acoustic and electric guitar.

poor working conditions, and about the political situation of the time. He owned a number of Martin guitars and wrote on many of them 'This machine kills fascists'!

Guthrie had a great influence on the young Bob Dylan (b.1941), who visited Guthrie when he was in hospital in the early 1960s. With his unique blend of piercing and heartfelt poetry, rasping voice and charisma, Dylan is perhaps the most important figure in the development of rock music, and had an incalculable influence on many other great rock artists such as the Rolling Stones and Jimi Hendrix.

Dylan started out singing standard folk and blues songs, accompanying himself on acoustic guitar and harmonica. He then started writing his own folk, blues and protest songs such as 'Blowin' in the Wind', which became universal anthems for a disaffected generation. In 1965 he turned to electric guitar along with a backing band, amid much controversy and incomprehension. Throughout his career, all of Dylan's many influences have surfaced at one time or another, including an acoustic revival.

INTRODUCTION: STAIRWAY TO HEAVEN

Words and music by Jimmy Page and Robert Plant

So just as Django had done in the jazz world, Dylan did in the folk world – but Dylan was also reaching out to a new stratosphere, creating his own brand of rock. One of the definitive rock bands of the 1970s was Led Zeppelin, who had phenomenal success with their albums. The band members also had folk leanings and their guitarist Jimmy Page often played acoustic guitar – shown to stunning effect in 'Stairway to Heaven', one of the most popular rock songs of all time. This starts off with a haunting melody on solo acoustic guitar and then takes off, with a switch to electric guitar, into the loud, frantic but still melodic world of hard rock. The musical notation for the introduction appears opposite.

The force of flamenco

And so we return to the Old World, to where the guitar had dug its deepest roots – Spain. Andalucia in the south of Spain was the last bastion of the Moors, who had controlled much of the country for almost 800 years, until 1492. Andalucia is where many immigrants had arrived from the East, some from as far as India. Flamenco is the name given to the folk music from Andalucia, which is sung, danced and accompanied by guitars. Flamenco music contains the inextricable influences of the Middle East, Moorish North Africa and Europe. The body and hand movements of the dancers are reminiscent of Indian and North African dance, and the singing is reminiscent of Middle Eastern religious chants. Rhythms include elements of the European Baroque, and some harmonies are based on Arabic scales.

Where the guitar was once servant to the singer and dancer, various outstanding players in the 20th century have presented the flamenco guitar as a solo instrument, drawing on all the elements described above, and transforming the instrument into a virtuoso vehicle. Players such as Ramón Montoya, Sabicas (born Agustín Castellón Campos) and Paco de Lucía, included tremolos, very fast scale passages, intricate arpeggios, and especially various types of *rasgueados* (a

LEFT Although as a band Led Zeppelin belonged in the 'hard rock' category, lead guitarist Jimmy Page often played acoustic guitar – most famously in the song 'Stairway to Heaven'.

ABOVE Exotic elements in flamenco from India and Moorish North Africa are embodied in the dance movement of this flamenco dancer in a work entitled 'El Jaleo' (1882), painted by American artist John Singer Sargent (1856–1925).

continuous strumming sound on the strings produced by rapid up-and-down finger movements), all played finger-style.

Flamenco guitars are very similar to classical guitars in appearance and construction, although the back and sides are made of a lighter Spanish cypress wood to produce a more percussive and incisive quality of sound. This is particularly suited to playing the explosive *rasgueados*. Solo flamenco guitar playing has gradually developed a distinctive personality of its own. Unleashed from the strictures of accompanying, guitarists have treated rhythmic and harmonic formulas with freedom and fantasy, producing music of great strength and individuality.

In closing: this survey of other guitar styles has not included the solid-body electric guitar, which has dominated commercial music for many years. That is a story worthy of a whole book in itself.

Looking at the overall development of the guitar in all its different forms and musical styles – classical, acoustic, and electric – and at its impact on music, culture and society, few could deny that the 20th century was indeed a golden age.

FLAMENCO (BASIC COMPÁS)

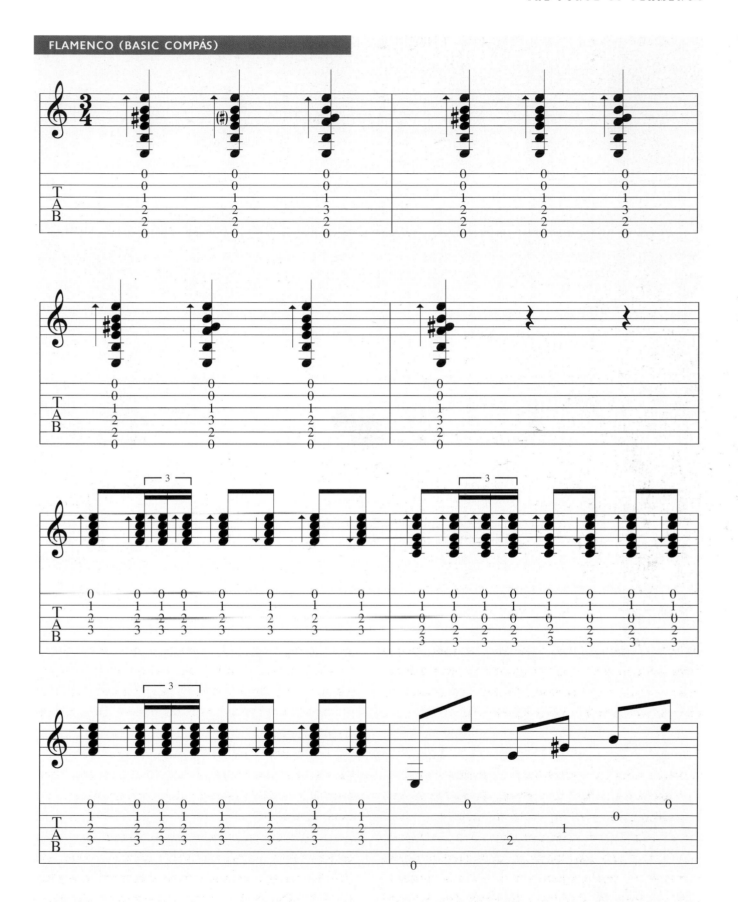

chapter five

FURTHER PLAYING AND LISTENING

Four leading guitarists greatly influenced guitar playing in the second part of the 20th century. They were Andrés Segovia (1893–1987), Alirio Díaz (b.1923), Julian Bream (b.1933) and John Williams (b.1941) — see their profiles later in this chapter. A direct line connects three of them: Alirio Díaz was a student of Segovia, and John Williams was a student of both. Julian Bream, who was 15 years old when Andrés Segovia was 55, also received help and encouragement from the older maestro.

Each of these guitarists made a profound impact in his own way. Segovia lit a torch which the other players picked up in locations across the globe: Alirio Díaz in Venezuela, Julian Bream in England and John Williams in Australia. Born and bred in such different locations, each guitarist brought to the instrument different experiences and cultural attitudes. The aspects they all had in common were their ability to connect and communicate with the listener, their contribution to the significant expansion of the repertoire, and the excellence of their playing.

There are considerable similarities in the techniques of Segovia, Díaz and Williams. In their right-hand technique, all three play with an elevated wrist and strongly curved thumb. They employ a mixture of free stroke and rest stroke (see Chapter 2), accommodated within a stable hand position. All three use a nail-based technique, with the left side of the nail approaching the string at an oblique angle. Julian Bream, perhaps less under the influence of Segovia, developed a more distinctive technique, also based on nail playing, with fingers and thumb stretched across the strings in opposite directions, and the fingers playing the strings deep on the inner left side of the nails.

The artistic and musical personalities of these artists are very different. Alirio Díaz plays continuous streams of notes with energy and excitement; Julian Bream searches for the inner expression of each moment; John Williams concentrates on clarity of phrasing and rhythmic precision.

Behind the dazzling virtuosity of these players lies a deep understanding of theory and harmony, so let us now make a brief survey of the 'science' of music.

RIGHT Julian Bream's interest in music for the guitar has extended from the 16th-century composers to the present day. He has been quoted as saying: 'I just happen to play the lute and the guitar – I feel my calling was simply to be a musician.'

INTERVALS AND SCALES

Intervals

The difference in pitch between two notes is known as the interval between the two notes.

Semitone interval

This is the interval between two adjacent notes. A semitone on the guitar is one fret. For example, if you press the first fret on a string and play the note, then press the second fret and play the note, the interval is one semitone.

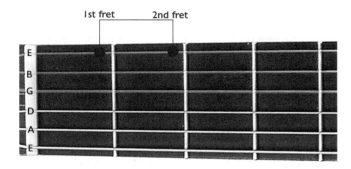

Tone interval

This is a difference of two adjacent semitones. A tone on the guitar is two frets. If you press the first fret and play the note, then press the third fret and play the note, the interval is one tone.

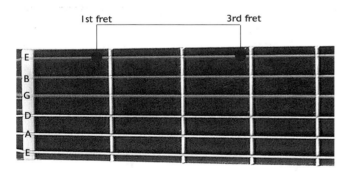

An octave

To briefly recap, the seven notes are named according to the first seven letters of the alphabet. The note that follows the 7th note, G, is again called A – and is termed the 8th note, and so on. The second note A is an octave apart from the first note A. The interval consists of a gap of 6 tones, or 12 semitones. So, if you play the open string and then press the 12th fret, the interval between those two notes is one octave. The two notes sound the same

but at a different pitch, the higher note vibrating at twice the frequency of the lower note. This is just as men and women naturally sing the same note, although they are singing an octave apart – the reason for the two notes having the same name.

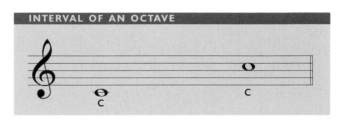

The scale

A scale is a consecutive series of notes framed by the octave. If you divide the octave into as many equal steps as possible you have 12 semitones. This is called a 'chromatic scale'.

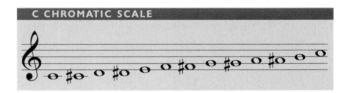

The name of the scale is taken from the octave notes. The interval between consecutive notes in the chromatic scale is a semitone (represented by two frets next to one another).

The octave can also be divided into unequal steps, by 'missing' a semitone. The major scale has only 8 notes, and so is missing some semitones.

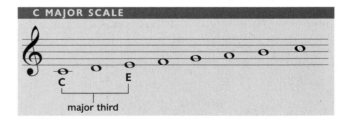

The consecutive gaps between the notes of the C major scale above are tone, tone, semitone, tone, tone, tone, semitone. If we divide the octave into a different arrangement of tones and semitones – tone, semitone, tone, tone, tone, tone, semitone – it is called the 'C melodic minor scale'.

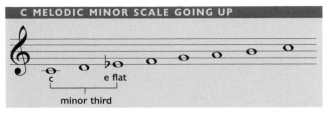

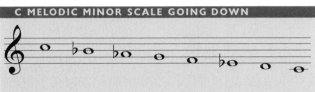

When this scale is played backward, in other words, from the highest note down to the lowest note, a pleasing melodic effect is created by changing the arrangement of tones and semitones between the highest three notes of the scale

Major and minor third intervals

The main difference between a major and a minor scale is the third note of the scale. In the minor, this third note is a semitone below that of the major, giving the minor scale a darker, more tragic sound. Here, the interval between the first and third notes is known as a 'minor third'. For example, in the C melodic minor scale above, the interval between C and E flat (also known as D sharp) is a minor third. Major scales generally sound bright and cheerful. The interval between the first and third notes of a major scale is a 'major third'. For example, in the C major scale opposite, the interval between C and E is a major third.

Other basic intervals

Intervals in a major or minor scale are named according to their relationship with the first note of the scale. The interval between the first and second notes of the scale is called a 'second'. As described above, that between the first and third notes is called a 'third', and can be major or minor. The interval between the first and fourth notes is a 'fourth', and similarly we have a 'fifth', a 'sixth' and a 'seventh', until finally the interval between the first and eighth notes is the octave interval as described above.

Harmonics

When you play a note, a set of vibrations is produced. The strongest vibration is along the entire length of string, which is called the 'fundamental'. Further vibrations are produced as multiples of the frequency of the fundamental: along half, a third, a quarter, a fifth, etc. of the length of string. These vibrations are referred to as the 'harmonic series', and each harmonic is called a 'partial', or an 'overtone'.

Where the strongest sounding note is the fundamental, the next strongest is the partial that sounds at half its length, followed by the partial that sounds at a third of its length, and so on. When you play the guitar you may be able to hear some partials quite clearly, whereas on some other instruments, for example the flute, they are more difficult to hear.

The partials can be sounded separately on the guitar by lightly touching the string at the 12th, 9th, 7th, 5th and 4th frets among others.

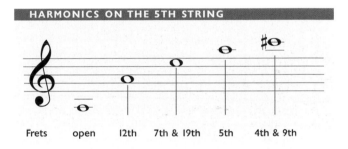

This is how the fretboard (fingerboard) corresponds to the notes of the harmonic series. Let us assume that the fundamental note is the open 5th string, A (see example above):

- the first overtone is sounded by dividing the string in half, at the 12th fret
- the second overtone is sounded by dividing the string in three, at the 7th and 19th frets (the same note is played at either fret)
- the third overtone is sounded by dividing the string in four, at the 5th fret
- the fourth overtone is sounded by dividing the string in five, at the 4th and 9th frets

Here are the intervals (the difference in pitch of each note) of the harmonic series based on the fundamental:

- the first overtone is one octave above, i.e. the note A
- the second overtone is one octave plus a fifth above, i.e. the note E
- the third overtone is two octaves above, i.e. the note A
- the fourth overtone is two octaves plus a major third above, i.e. the note C#.

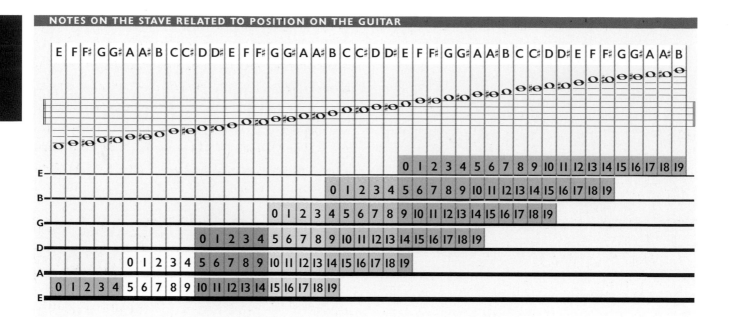

NOTES ON THE STAVE RELATED TO POSITION ON THE GUITAR

Tips on playing the harmonics

- Use the flat part of the left-hand finger, not the tip.
- Rest the finger very lightly over the fret itself, so as to touch the string but not press it down onto a fret.
- Play the note strongly with the right hand, halfway between the sound hole and the bridge.
- Immediately after sounding the note, release the left-hand finger.

Practice

Play the 'Spanish Bugle Call' on p26 using the same rhythm and sequence of strings – but this time, instead of playing the notes on the open strings, play the notes in harmonics at the 12th fret. Repeat the exercise, this time playing the notes in harmonics at the 5th fret.

Transposition and keys

The three scales already discussed (chromatic, major and minor) are all framed by the octave. So far, the octave frame used as a model has been based on the note C.

What would you have to do if you wanted to play the scales starting on, say, the note G? Provided you used the same corresponding series of intervals between the notes for each scale, then you would be playing a G chromatic scale, a G major scale, and a G melodic minor scale. These patterns of notes form a model that can start on any note; the musical term used is 'transposition'.

G chromatic scale

In the C chromatic scale, you divided the octave into as many equal steps as possible. Each step represented a semitone, or one fret. You can do the same with the G chromatic scale, by dividing the octave in the same way, based on and starting on the note G.

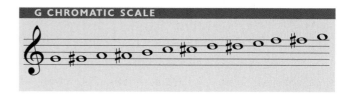

G CHROMATIC SCALE

G major scale

If you want to play a major scale framed by the octave notes G, then you can do so by keeping the same gaps between the notes as the scale starting on C. These consecutive gaps were tone, tone, semitone, tone, tone, tone, semitone. If you do the same starting on G, you play a G major scale (see below).

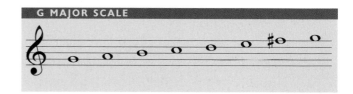

G MAJOR SCALE

G melodic minor scale

In the G melodic minor scale, keep to the same arrangement of consecutive gaps as the scale on C, but start on G.

To play the melodic minor in the G scale going down (see below), you follow the same changes as in the C version.

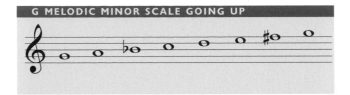

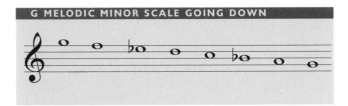

Key and key signature

When you play a scale of G major, you are playing in the 'key' of G major; similarly when you're playing a scale of G minor, you're playing in the key of G minor. A piece or section of music based on the notes of the G major or G minor scale is also referred to as being in the key of G major or G minor. At the beginning of a piece of music, the sharps and flats denote the key of the piece. This is called the 'key signature'; it is placed after the treble clef and before the time signature.

ALIRIO DÍAZ

Alirio Díaz was born in 1923 in La Candelabria, a tiny village in the arid desert of mid-Venezuela. Díaz studied literature, history of art, and philosophy in the nearest large town, Carora (6000 inhabitants), and one of the earliest settlements of the Spanish *conquistadores*. Don Cecilio Zubillaga Perera, the renowned local teacher, encouraged him to pursue his musical studies, which he did in Caracas, eventually travelling to Madrid with his fellow student Rodrigo Riera, guitarist and future composer of 'Cancion Caroreña'.

Like many Venezuelan musicians, Díaz began his musical studies on the *cuatro* – a four-string instrument in the shape of a guitar, but only slightly larger than a mandolin. The child-friendly size of the instrument encouraged technical freedom, and a quick entry into chords and syncopated rhythmical accompaniments in the folk style. The structure of these folk dances encourages improvisation and virtuosity.

Whilst in Caracas, Díaz developed an association with leading musicians of the time including composers Antonio Lauro (1917–1986) and Vicente Sojo (1887–1974). Their music was to feature large in his repertoire. He edited and arranged much of their

ABOVE Carlos Bonell presents Alirio Díaz with John Williams' CD of Venezuelan music on his 80th birthday, in 2003.

music, as well as making his own arrangements of music by other Venezuelan composers, whose folk roots shone through all they composed.

As he established an international career playing the mainstream repertoire, he continued to play and promote the music of his native land – and so brought this exuberant music to widespread international attention. Headlong rushes of notes were dispatched with brilliance and infinite shades of rhythmic subtlety.

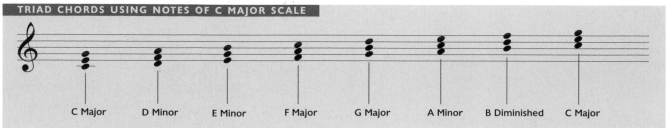

TRIAD CHORDS USING NOTES OF C MAJOR SCALE

C Major · D Minor · E Minor · F Major · G Major · A Minor · B Diminished · C Major

CHORDS AND ARPEGGIOS

A 'chord' is a group of notes played simultaneously, producing a pleasing sound. The minimum number of notes in a chord is three, called a 'triad', and it is based on major and minor scales. By taking any note of a scale and adding the third and fifth step (called 'degree') above it, you form a chord.

Using the notes of the C major scale as an example: take the note C itself, and add the third and fifth degree of the scale above it: E and G respectively. Take another note of the scale, for example D. Add the third and fifth degree of the scale: F and A. The example above shows all the triad chords based on the scale of C with the names of the chords.

When you play the notes of a triad or chord one after the other rather than simultaneously, you are playing an 'arpeggio' (see example below).

C MAJOR ARPEGGIO & CHORD IN 1ST POSITION

The chord of C major can be played in 1st position with 5 notes – consisting of the triad of C major plus 2 additional notes: another C and another E (see example above).

Basic chord patterns in 1st position

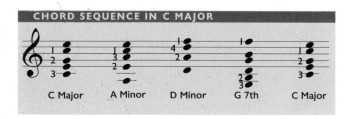

CHORD SEQUENCE IN C MAJOR

C Major · A Minor · D Minor · G 7th · C Major

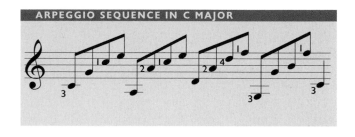

ARPEGGIO SEQUENCE IN C MAJOR

Transposing chord patterns

Chord patterns in 1st position can be transposed into different positions on the guitar, enabling you to play chords in many different keys using the same fingering pattern.

In some of the transposed chord patterns, the left-hand index finger acts as a capo, or movable nut. The index finger lies flat on the fretboard, covering from 2 to 6 strings. This is called 'barré' technique and requires understanding, skill and practice to use it effectively.

As an exercise, transpose the chord shape of E major as in the example below – see figure (A).

Then rearrange the fingering pattern as indicated below in figure (B).

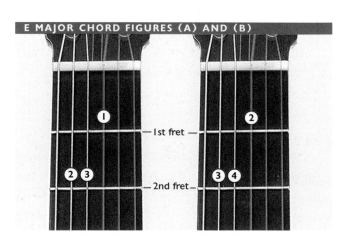

E MAJOR CHORD FIGURES (A) AND (B)

1st fret · 2nd fret

Slide fingers up one fret, so that the second finger is on the 2nd fret, and the third and fourth fingers on the 3rd fret. Place the index finger in barré position across the 6 strings of the 1st fret, as indicated at right. You are now playing the chord of F major.

You can slide the same shape up all the way to the 10th fret, and so can play the chords of F, F#, G, G#, A, A#, B, C, C# and D major, using the same fingering pattern.

F MAJOR CHORD

1st fret

2nd fret

3rd fret

JULIAN BREAM

Julian Bream was born in Battersea, in the heart of London, in 1933. His first teacher was his father who played the plectrum jazz guitar. His interests in music developed in three directions: the Renaissance lute, the standard guitar repertoire and the creation of a new guitar repertoire. Where Segovia had cultivated an axis of composers mostly from Spain and Latin America, Bream extended the range to include some of the leading composers of the day. From Britain they included the likes of Sir Peter Maxwell Davies and Benjamin Britten. Others who composed works for him were Hans Werner Henze from Germany, Toru Takemitsu from Japan, and Leo Brouwer from Cuba.

For many of these composers it was the first time they had composed for the instrument, and so brought to it a fresh, unclichéd approach. With Segovia setting the precedent for composers unfamiliar with the guitar, Julian Bream similarly acted as inspirer, collaborating as editor and arranger if necessary. With Bream's dedication to the cause of new music for the guitar, and his promotion of it through performances and recordings, the instrument acquired a gleaming new image of modernity, and each new Bream première became a special occasion to look forward to.

Even while rediscovering forgotten lute music and pushing forward the boundaries of new music, Julian Bream was still able to delve deeply into the guitar repertoire, including Segovia's, and present it newly minted and shining. His amazing ear for the sonority of the instrument, his ability to finely balance chord voicings, to create exquisite tone, and to imbue every phrase with an inner life assured him a pre-eminent position in the musical world.

BELOW Julian Bream led the Early Music revival on the lute, and commissioned new guitar music from leading composers.

E MINOR CHORD FIGURES (A) AND (B)

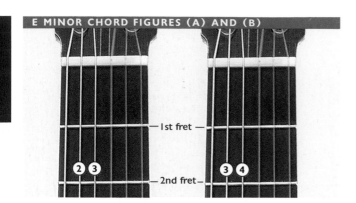

Now try transposing the chord shape of E minor – see above example (A).

Rearrange the fingering pattern as indicated in (B) above.

F MINOR CHORD

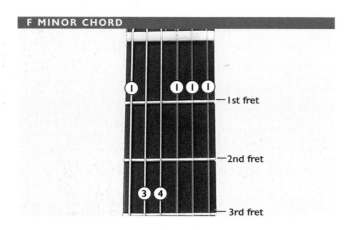

Slide your fingers up one fret, with barré, as described on p78. You can slide the same shape up all the way to the 10th fret to play the chords of F, F#, G, G#, A, A#, B, C, C# and D minor, using the same fingering configuration (see diagram above).

A MAJOR CHORD FIGURES (A) AND (B)

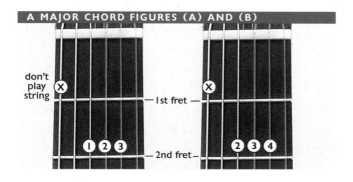

Transpose the chord shape of A major – see (A) above.
Rearrange the fingering pattern as indicated in example (B).

A# MAJOR CHORD

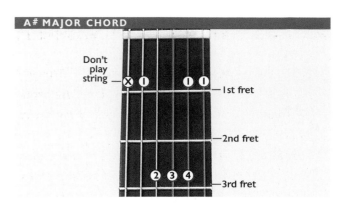

Slide fingers up one fret, with barré, as earlier (see example above). You can slide the same shape up all the way to the 10th fret to play the chords of A#, B, C, C#, D, D#, E, F, F#, and G major.

A MINOR CHORD FIGURES (A) AND (B)

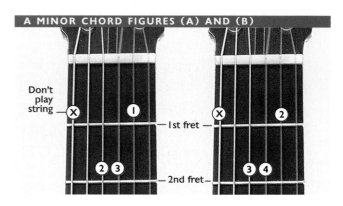

Transpose the chord shape of A minor – see example (A) above. Rearrange the fingering pattern as in (B) above.

A# MINOR CHORD

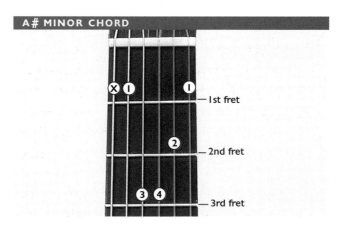

Slide fingers up one fret, with barré. You can then slide the same shape up all the way to the 10th fret to play the chords of A#, B, C, C#, D, D#, E, F, F#, and G minor.

JOHN WILLIAMS

Born in Melbourne, Australia, in 1941, John Williams moved to England when he was 11 years old. He began his studies with his father and continued them with Alirio Díaz and Andrés Segovia.

His playing as a young man had an immediate impact — the impression given was of a flawless technique at the service of a fluid understated musicality, projected through a sound world derived from Segovia. The difference lay in that where Segovia altered rhythm and phrasing to suit an expressive effect, Williams incorporated expression into a seamless rhythmic fabric. This feature became his trademark: John Williams' playing was water to Segovia's fire. In the same vein of comparison, Julian Bream was earth and Alirio Díaz wind!

Since the 1960s, Williams has been at the vanguard of breaking down the barriers between musical styles, and of reaching new audiences. This led to the formation of John Williams and Friends in 1974, of which the author was a member. His lifelong interest in world music takes in Chile, Venezuela, Africa, and his native Australia. He presents concerts and makes recordings with local musicians, and has created various dedicated ensembles.

Throughout his career, he has encouraged composers whose work is more usually associated with commercial music to compose for him. The results include the group Sky, the famous 'Cavatina' by Stanley Myers — universally known as the theme from the film *The Deer Hunter*, and a concerto from André Previn. At the same time, Williams relishes exploring the more conventional repertoire. He has championed newly discovered works by the Paraguayan composer Agustín Barrios, and the music of contemporary composers Toru Takemitsu, Stephen Dodgson and many others. John Williams has an unrivalled skill for communicating musical ideas with total clarity and

ABOVE John Williams has set new standards of excellence. He once said, 'The guitar can be the bridge between the popular and classical traditions'.

perfect technique. His wide musical curiosity has, too, matured him into a guitarist deeply immersed in different styles, the influence of which is reflected in the breadth and depth of his expressive playing.

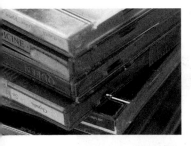

RECOMMENDED RECORDINGS LIST

Medieval Age c.400–1500AD

Performed by: Unicorn Ensemble
Composer: Alfonso X 'el Sabio' et al
Title: *Cantigas de Santa María*
Label: Naxos

Performed by: Perceval Ensemble
Composer: Richard the Lionheart, Alfonso X et al
Title: *Songs of Kings and Princes of the Middle Ages*
Label: Arion

Performed by: Perceval Ensemble
Composer: Adam de la Halle
Title: *(Le) Jeu de Robin et de Marion*
Label: Arion

Performed by: Andrew Lawrence-King, Paul Hillier
Composers: Martin Codax and Jaufre Rudel
Title: *Distant Love – Songs of Martin Codax and Jaufre Rudel*
Label: Harmonia Mundi

Performed by: Paul Hillier, Andrew Lawrence-King
Composers: Thibault de Champagne, Gace Brulé, Moniot d'Arras, Colin Muset, Anon
Title: *French Troubadour Songs*
Label: Harmonia Mundi

Performed by: Sequentia
Composer: Hildegard von Bingen
Title: *Canticles of Ecstasy*
Label: Deutsche Harmonia Mundi

Music for vihuela

Performed by: Julian Bream
Composers (for vihuela): Mudarra, Milan, Narvaez, Boccherini, Tarrega, Sor
Title: *Music of Spain – Guitarra, Julian Bream Edition, Vol. 27*
Label: BMG Classics

Performed by: Andrés Segovia
Composers: Milan, Sanz, Roncalli, Aguado, Sor, Granados, Bach, Ponce, Albéniz, Murcia, Rodrigo, Mompou, Castelnuovo-Tedesco, Moreno Torroba, Espla, Boccherini
Title: *Segovia – The Collection*
Label: Deutsche Grammophon

Performed by: Hopkinson Smith
Composer: Luys de Narváez
Title: *Narváez: Los seys libros del Delphin de música*
Label: Astrée

Performed by: Andrew Watts, Andrew Lawrence-King (harp) et al; Westminster Cathedral Choir
Composers: Padilla, Salazar, Franco, Capillas
Title: *Masterpieces of Mexican Polyphony*
Label: Hyperion

The lute and Dowland

Performed by: Julian Bream
Composers: Dowland, Byrd, Cutting, Rosseter, John Johnson, Bulman, Bacheler, Holborne, Robert Johnson
Title: *Golden Age of English Lute Music, Julian Bream Edition, Vol. 1*
Label: RCA

Performed by: Jakob Lindberg, Nigel North, Anthony Rooley, Christopher Wilson, Emma Kirkby et al
Composer: John Dowland
Title: *Dowland: Collected Works*
Label: L'Oiseau-Lyre

Baroque guitar

Performed by: John Williams
Composer: Johann Sebastian Bach
Title: *Bach – Transcriptions for Guitar*
Label: Sony Classical

Performed by: King's Consort
Composer: Henry Purcell
Title: *Complete Odes and Welcome Songs, Vol. 1–8*
Label: Hyperion

Performed by: Andrés Segovia
Segovia – The Collection (see p82)

Performed by: Andrés Segovia
Composers: Visée; Galilei, Bach, Tansman et al
Title: *Segovia*
Label: BBC Legends

Performed by: Julian Bream
Composers: Sanz, Visée, Weiss, Sor, Bach
Title: *Baroque Guitar*
Label: RCA Classics

Performed by: Julian Bream
Composers: Sanz, Visée, Weiss, Bach, Frescobaldi, Scarlatti, Guerau, Cimarosa
Title: *Julian Bream Edition, Vol. 9: Baroque Guitar*
Label: RCA Gold Seal

Spain and folk music

Performed by: Julian Bream
Composer: Sanz, de Visée, Weiss, Sor, Bach
Title: *Baroque Guitar*
Label: RCA Classics

Performed by: Julian Bream
Title: *Julian Bream Edition, Vol. 9: Baroque Guitar* (see above)

Performed by: Andrés Segovia
Title: *Segovia – The Collection* (see p82)

Classical guitar

Performed by: Julian Bream (lute)
Title: *Music of Spain – Guitarra* (see p82)

Paganini & the Italian connection

Performed by: Julian Bream and John Williams
Composers: Giuliani, Carulli, Granados, Albéniz, John Johnson, Telemann, Debussy
Title: *Together Again – Julian Bream and John Williams*
Label: RCA Gold Seal

Performed by: Pepe Romero & Academy of St Martin-in-the-Fields
Composers: Carulli, Mozart, Molino
Title: *Carulli: Guitar Concertos*
Label: Philips

Performed by: Julian Bream
Composers: Giuliani, Sor
Title: *Julian Bream Edition, Vol. 10: Classic Guitar*
Label: RCA Victor (discontinued)

The Romantic Age

Performed by: Andrés Segovia
Composers: Tárrega, Albéniz, Moreno Torroba, Rodrigo, Ponce, Castelnuovo-Tedesco, Villa-Lobos, Turina, Sor, Roussel, Debussy, Segovia, Bach et al
Title: *The Art of Segovia*
Label: Deutsche Grammophon

Performed by: Julian Bream
Composers: Tárrega, Paganini, Falla, Albéniz, Debussy, Schubert, Mendelssohn

Title: *Julian Bream Edition, Vol. 11: Romantic Guitar*
Label: RCA

Albéniz, Granados & the guitar

Performed by: Andrés Segovia
Composers: Granados, Albéniz, Bach, Turina,
Moreno Torroba, Ponce, Castelnuovo-Tedesco,
Malats et al
Title: *The Legendary Segovia*
Label: EMI Classics

Performed by: John Williams
Composer: Isaac Albéniz
Title: *Albéniz-Guitar Works*
Label: Sony Classics

Performed by: Julian Bream and John Williams
Composers: Giuliani, Carulli, Granados, Albéniz,
John Johnson, Telemann, Debussy
Title: *Together Again – Julian Bream and John
Williams*
Label: RCA Gold Seal

Performed by: Dario Rossetti-Bonell
Composers: Granados, Villa-Lobos, Barrios,
Vivaldi
Title: *Music for Guitar*
Label: EMI Classics

Transition to the 20th century

Performed by: Julian Bream
Composers: Pujol, Llobet, Tárrega, Turina
Title: *Julian Bream Edition, Vol. 26 – Music of Spain*
Label: RCA

Performed by: Andrés Segovia
Title: *The Art of Segovia* (see p83)

Performed by: Andrés Segovia
Composers: Tansman, Bach, Visée, Galilei, Schubert,
Villa-Lobos, Castelnuovo-Tedesco

Title: *Segovia*
Label: BBC Legends
(Also: recordings by Andrés Segovia of: Ponce,
Granados, Sor, Moreno Torroba)

Performed by: John Williams
Composers: Ponce, Rodrigo, Vivaldi, Giuliani, Villa-
Lobos, Castelnuovo-Tedesco
Title: *The Great Guitar Concertos*
Label: Masterworks

Performed by: John Williams
Composers: Bach, Scarlatti, Albéniz, Ponce, Sor,
Segovia, Tansman, Granados, Lauro
Title: *John Williams – Guitar Recital*
Label: Double Decca

Performed by: John Williams
Composers: Barrios, Ponce
Title: *Latin-American Guitar Music by Barrios
and Ponce*
Label: Essential Classics

Performed by: Julian Bream
Composers: Roussel, Walton, Berkeley, Smith
Brindle, Henze, Martin, Rawsthorne
Title: *Julian Bream Edition, Vol. 12: 20th-Century
Guitar I*
Label: RCA Victor

20th-century composers

Performed by: Andrés Segovia
Title: *The Legendary Segovia* (see above)

Performed by: John Williams
Composers: Rodrigo, Llobet, Albéniz, Granados
Title: *Iberia – John Williams Plays Music of Spain*
Label: Sony Classical

Performed by: Julian Bream
Composers: Tárrega, Paganini, de Falla, Albéniz,

Debussy, Schubert, Mendelssohn
Title: *Julian Bream Edition, Vol. II: Romantic Guitar*
Label: RCA

Performed by: Julian Bream
Composers: Joaquín Rodrigo
Title: *Julian Bream Edition, Vol. 28 – Music of Spain*
Label: RCA

Performed by: Chick Corea and Return to Forever
Composer: Joaquín Rodrigo
Title: *Light As a Feather* [original recording remastered]
Label: Verve

Performed by: Montreal Symphony Orchestra with Carlos Bonell & Alicia de Larrocha
Composers: Rodrigo, Falla, Albéniz, Turina
Title: *Concierto de Aranjuez/Spanish Orchestral Works*
Label: Decca

Performed by: Miles Davis
Composer: Joaquín Rodrigo (arranged by Davis)
Title: *Sketches of Spain*
Label: Sony Jazz

Performed by: John Williams, Daniel Barenboim, Sir Charles Groves, English Chamber Orchestra
Composers: Castelnuovo-Tedesco, Rodrigo, Villa-Lobos
Title: *Guitar Concertos*
Label: Sony Classics (discontinued)

Performed by: John Williams
Composer: Agustín Barrios
Title: *The Great Paraguayan*
Label: Sony Classical

Barrios plays Barrios
Various archive collections available

Performed by: Julian Bream
Composer: Heitor Villa-Lobos
Title: *Julian Bream Edition, Vol. 21: Villa-Lobos*
Label: RCA Gold Seal

Performed by: Heitor Villa-Lobos, French Radio Chorus, French Radio National Orchestra
Composer: Villa-Lobos et al
Title: *Villa-Lobos conducts Villa-Lobos*
Label: EMI

20th century music of a different kind

Performed by: John Williams
Composer: Leo Brouwer
Title: *Black Decameron – the Music of Leo Brouwer*
Label: Sony Classical

Performed by: John Williams
Title: *The Great Guitar Concertos* (see p84)

Performed by: John Williams
Composer: Toru Takemitsu
Title: *John Williams Plays Music of Takemitsu*
Label: Sony Classical

Performed by: John Williams and Timothy Kain
Composers: Brouwer, Houghton, Hand, Takemitsu, Verdery, Shostakovich, Westlake, Madlem, Bellinati, O'Carolan, Soler, Granados
Title: *The Mantis and the Moon – Music for Two Guitars*

Performed by: Pablo Sainz Villegas et al
Composer: Luciano Berio
Title: *The Complete Sequenzas for Solo Instruments* (incl. guitar Sequenza)
Label: Naxos

Performed by: Patricia Rozario, Eileen Hulse, Heidi Grant-Murphy, et al
Composer: John Tavener

Title: *John Tavener – a Portrait*
Label: Naxos Educational

Performed by: Julian Bream
Composers: Britten, Martin, Brouwer, Takemitsu, Lutoslawski
Title: *Nocturnal*
Label: Emi Classical (discontinued)

Composers: Roussel, Walton, Berkeley, Smith Brindle, Henze, Martin, Rawsthorne
Title: *Julian Bream Edition, Vol. 12: 20th-Century Guitar I*
Label: RCA Victor (discontinued)

Alirio Díaz

Performed by: Alirio Díaz
Title: *Five Centuries of Spanish Guitar Music*
Label: Legacy

Blues and Jazz

Performed by: Duke Ellington
Title: *The Centenary Collection*
Label: Pulse

Performed by: Count Basie
Title: *The Count Basie Story*
Label: Proper

Performed by: Benny Goodman, Charlie Christian
Title: *The Benny Goodman sextet featuring Charlie Christian*
Label: Sony

Performed by: Benny Goodman and his Orchestra
Title: series of CDs covering different years
Label: Classics

Performed by: Robert Johnson
Title: *King of the Delta Blues Singers*
Label: Legacy

Performed by: Big Bill Broonzy
Title: *Big Bill's Blues*
Label: Topaz

Performed by: Blind Lemon Jefferson
Title: *The Complete 94 Classic Sides Remastered*
Label: JSP

Performed by: Lightnin' Hopkins
Title: *Lightnin' Hopkins*
Label: Smithsonian Folkways

Performed by: Joe Pass
Title: *Guitar Virtuoso*
Label: Pablo

Django Reinhardt and Gypsy jazz

Performed by: Django Reinhardt
Title: *Swing de Paris*
Label: Proper Box

Performed by: Le Quintette du Hot Club de France
Title: *25 Classics 1934–1940*
Label: ASV Living Era

João Gilberto and bossa nova

Performed by: João Gilberto
Title: *Live in Montreux*
Label: Elektra

Performed by: Antonio Carlos Jobim, João Gilberto, Astrud Gilberto, Luiz Bonfa, Stan Getz, Ella Fitzgerald, Dizzy Gillespie, Oscar Peterson, Charlie Byrd, Wes Montgomery, Billy Eckstine, Sarah Vaughan and Shirley Horn
Title: *The Antonio Carlos Jobim Songbook*
Label: Verve

Performed by: Stan Getz, Charlie Byrd
Title: *Jazz Samba*
Label: Verve

From folk to pop and rock

Performed by: Woody Guthrie
Title: *The Very Best of Woody Guthrie*
Label: Music Club

Performed by: Bob Dylan
Title: *The Essential Bob Dylan*
Label: Sony Music TV

Performed by: Simon & Garfunkel
Title: *Parsley, Sage, Rosemary and Thyme*
Label: Columbia

Performed by: Nick Drake
Title: *Five Leaves Left*
Label: Island

Performed by: Stefan Grossman, John Renbourne
Title: *Under the Volcano*
Label: Kicking Mule

Performed by: Joni Mitchell
Title: *Blue*
Label: Warner

Performed by: Led Zeppelin
Title: *Led Zeppelin III & Led Zeppelin IV*
Label: Warner

Performed by: Eric Clapton
Title: *Unplugged*
Label: Warner

Performed by: Nirvana
Title: *Unplugged in New York*
Label: Geffen

Performed by: Sting
Title: *Sacred Love*
Label: A&M

The force of flamenco

Performed by: Ramón Montoya
Title: *Flamenco – L'Art de Ramón Montoya 1924–36*
Label: Fremeaux

Performed by: Sabicas
Title: *Flamenco on Fire*
Label: Legacy

Performed by: Carlos Montoya
Title: *The Art of Flamenco*
Label: Laserlight

Performed by: Paco de Lucía
Title: *Live in America*
Label: Polydor

Performed by: Radio Tarifa
Title: *Cruzando el Rio*
Label: World Circuit

Performed by: Paco Peña
Title: *Fabulous Flamenco*
Label: London

ABOVE: John Williams has had an enormous influence on modern guitar music. Embracing many different styles, his playing has extended to rock, film soundtracks and orchestra.

chapter six

GLOSSARY

Action: The action is the height of the string from the fingerboard. It is usually measured at the 12th fret.

Arpeggio: Playing the notes of a chord one after the other, rather than simultaneously.

Atonality: A form of music that defies the convention of centering music on one key. Instead of there being a 'home base' to which the music returns, all notes have equal validity, as do all possible sequences of notes and combinations of notes within chords.

Barré: Method of placing the index finger flat across the strings on the fretboard to hold down more than one note

Bottleneck slide: A glass, metal or plastic tube placed over the third or fourth finger of the left hand, used to create a fretless singing sound effect.

Capo: A removable device that is fixed to the fretboard to alter the pitch of the guitar.

Chord: A group of at least three notes played together.

Course: Pair of strings placed close together and played as one.

Fretboard or fingerboard: The area on the neck of the guitar on which the frets are placed. The terms fretboard and fingerboard can be used interchangeably.

Harmonics: The notes produced as multiples of the frequency of the fundamental (or lowest) vibration, when any note is played.

Interval: The difference in pitch between two notes.

Key: A key refers to the main scale pattern on which a piece of music is based. It takes its name from that scale pattern.

Metronome: A device that marks time – audibly, visually or both together.

Musical notation: Music written on a stave is referred to as musical notation.

Octave: A musical interval of eight notes, which encompasses 12 semi-tones.

Open string: A string that is played without using a finger to press the string to the fretboard.

p, i, m, a: The letters used on musical notation to indicate right-hand fingering. They are derived from the Spanish names for the thumb (*pulgar*), index finger (*indice*), middle finger (*medio*) and ring finger (*anular*).

Rasgueado: A rapid strumming motion of the right-hand fingers in quick succession, much used in flamenco music.

Sustain: The length of time a note will sound, or resonate, after a string has been plucked.

Semitone: The smallest interval between two notes, in Western music. On the fingerboard, a semitone is represented by adjacent frets.

Stave or staff: Music is written in notes on a stave, which consists of five parallel lines.

Tablature: A form of notation, being the graphic representation of the fingerboard where each line represents a string.

Tone: An interval of two semitones, represented on the guitar by a gap of one fret.

Transposition: Moving a sequence of notes in one key to another key, using the same corresponding sequence of intervals.

BIBLIOGRAPHY

Books

Tony Bacon (1991) *The Ultimate Guitar Book.* London: Dorling Kindersley.

Ralph Denyer (1992) *The Guitar Handbook.* London: Dorling Kindersley/Pan Books.

Richard Chapman (1993) *The Complete Guitarist.* London: Dorling Kindersley.

Geoffrey Hindley (1997) *Larousse Encyclopedia of Music.* New York: Smithmark Publishers.

Jose L. Romanillos, Julian Bream (Foreword) (1998) *Antonio De Torres, Guitar Maker: His Life and Work* (Yehudi Menuhin Music Guides). London: Kahn & Averill.

Eric Taylor (1991) *The AB Guide to Music Theory Parts 1 and 2.* London: The Associated Board of the Royal Schools of Music.

Frederick M. Noad (1997) *Playing the Guitar.* New York: Music Sales Corporation.

Barry Green, W. Timothy Gallwey (1986) *The Inner Game of Music.* New York: Anchor Books/Doubleday/Random House.

Leopold Auer (1980) *Violin Playing as I Teach it.* Mineola, NY: Dover Publications.

John Brande Trend (2001) *A Picture of Modern Spain: Men and Music.* Temecula, CA: Best Books.

Dr Paula Baillie-Hamilton (2004) *The Body Restoration Plan.* London: Penguin Books.

James Tyler (1980) *The Early Guitar: A History and Handbook* (Early Music Series). Oxford: Oxford University Press

Brian Jeffery (1994) *Fernando Sor: Composer and Guitarist.* London: Tecla Editions.

Tárrega: ensayo biográfico (1978) *Emilio Pujol.* Valencia: Artes Gráficas Soler.

Andrés Segovia, W.F. O'Brien (Translator) (1982) *Segovia: An Autobiography of the Years 1893–1920.* London: Marion Boyars Publishers.

Graham Wade (1982) *Traditions of the Classical Guitar.* London: Calder Publications Ltd.

Harvey Turnbull (1974) *The Guitar from the Renaissance to the Present Day.* Westport, CT: Bold Strummer Ltd.

Joaquín Rodrigo, Antonio Iglesias (1999) *Escritos de Joaquín Rodrigo.* Madrid: Editorial Alpuerto.

Victoria Kamhi de Rodrigo (1986) *De la mano de Joaquín Rodrigo: Historia de nuestra vida* (Colección Memorias de la música española). Madrid: Ediciones Joaquín Rodrigo.

Victoria Kamhi de Rodrigo, translated by Ellen Wilkerson (1992) *Hand in hand with Joaquín Rodrigo: My life at the Maestro's side* (English translation). Pittsburgh, PA: Latin American Literary Review Press.

Richard D. Stover (1992) *Six Silver Moonbeams: The Life and Times of Agustín Barrios Mangore.* Santa Fe, New Mexico: Querico Publications.

Deryck Cooke (1989) *The Language of Music.* Oxford: Clarendon Paperbacks/Oxford University Press.

Igor Stravinsky (1998) *Igor Stravinsky: An Autobiography.* New York: W. W. Norton & Company.

Websites

Guitarra Magazine
www.guitarramagazine.com

Archaeonia — A Journey through Ancient Greece
www.archaeonia.com

The Columbia Encyclopedia
www.bartleby.com/65/

Classical Guitar Illustrated History
www.classicalguitarmidi.com/history/

Fundación Victoria y Joaquín Rodrigo
www.joaquin-rodrigo.com

John Williams the Guitarist
plum.cream.org/williams

Spanish Guitar History
es.geocities.com/guitarraespanola/english.htm

INDEX

Entries in **bold** indicate photographs or illustrations

AUTHOR'S ACKNOWLEDGEMENTS

It has been a great pleasure to write this book, because it has obliged me to consider many aspects of playing and teaching the guitar. My main concern as a player is to communicate with the listener by providing an entertaining and educational experience. As a teacher I aim to do the same, and I hope this book communicates with the reader in a similar manner.
If you enjoy this book it will be due largely to the encouragement of many friends and colleagues who have urged me to put pen to paper. They must take the credit for giving me the confidence to do so.
Some of them have helped in very practical ways.

Chief among these is Julia Hickman, who not only researched invaluable material, but also made excellent suggestions, and improved much of my writing to create a smooth, flowing text. She also checked all the facts and dates, although any errors that may remain are entirely my responsibility. I could not have written the book without her unfailing support. Dario Rossetti-Bonell provided the excellent musical examples in the 'Other Styles' chapter for which I am very grateful, as well as giving me invaluable advice about different guitar styles. David Young gave me a historical overview of, and insights into, the popular guitar styles of the 20th century, which greatly helped focus my thoughts.

I am also extremely grateful to Jane Bentley, Ralph Desmarais, Terry Hennessey and Emma Rosa Oropeza de Herrera for their generous help and advice, and to my editors Simon Pooley, Alfred LeMaitre and Mariëlle Renssen, and designer Steven Felmore, for their patience, understanding and support from beginning to end. Conversations with the pianist and conductor Vladimir Ashkenazy, the conductor Rafael Frühbeck de Burgos, and the violinist Peter Fisher provided some unique opinions and anecdotes. I must mention three great friends whose writings have been an inspiration, and whose dedication to excellence was an example to follow. They are the composer Ottavio Négro, and the writers Leonor Peña and Pierluigi Lanza de Cristoforis. They gave me their time, and their answers to my many questions revealed extraordinary insights. Thank you all.

PHOTOGRAPHIC CREDITS

All photography copyright New Holland Image Library (NHIL)/Ryno Reyneke, with the exception of the following images (copyright rests with the individuals and/or their agencies as credited below).

pp2–3 NHIL/Duncan Soar; 4–5 NHIL/Duncan Soar; 10 Lebrecht Music & Arts; 14 (bottom right), 15 NHIL/Duncan Soar; 19 NHIL/Duncan Soar; 21 NHIL/Duncan Soar; 24 NHIL/Duncan Soar; 27 NHIL/Duncan Soar; 28–29 NHIL/Duncan Soar; 30 NHIL/Duncan Soar; 39 Peter Davies; 41 Bridgeman Art Library; 42 (top) Lebrecht Music Collection, (bottom) Lebrecht Music & Arts; 43 Private Collection/Lebrecht Music Collection 44 (top) Lebrecht Music & Arts; 44 (bottom) Lebrecht Music Collection; 46 Lebrecht Music & Arts; 47 (Ingres, Louvre, Paris) Bridgeman Art Library; 48 Lebrecht Music & Arts; 49 (inset) Private Collection/Lebrecht Music Collection, (bottom) Lebrecht Music Collection; 50 Lebrecht Music & Arts; 51 Opera News/Stageimage/Redferns; 52 (top) Carlos Bonell, (bottom) Archivo Manuel de Falla/Lebrecht; 53 Bridgeman Art Library; 54 Rico Stover; 55 (top) Lebrecht Music Collection, (bottom) Forum/Lebrecht Music & Arts; 56 G. Anderhub/Lebrecht Music Collection; 57 (top) Brian Seed/Lebrecht Music Collection, (bottom) Richard Haughton/Lebrecht Music; 58 (left) George Newson/Lebrecht Music, (right) Richard H. Smith/Lebrecht Music; 59 (top) Interfoto, Munich/Lebrecht Music Collection, (bottom) Lebrecht Music Collection; 61 Touchline Photo; 62 (inset) Private Collection/Lebrecht Music & Arts, (bottom) Michael Ochs Archives/Redferns; 64 Max Jones Files/Redferns; 65 William Gottlieb/Redferns; 67 (top) Toby Wales/Redferns, (bottom) Bob King/Redferns; 69 Grant Davis/Redferns; 70 Bridgeman Art Library; 73 David Redfern/Redferns; 77 Roberto Gonzalez (Venezuela); 79 David Farrell/Lebrecht Music Collection; 81 BBC/Redferns; 86–87 Sisi Burn/ArenaPAL